Camb

a travel surv

Daniel Robinson
Tony Wheeler

D1167865

Cambodia – a travel survival kit

1st edition

Published by
Lonely Planet Publications
Head Office: PO Box 617, Hawthorn, Vic 3122, Australia
Branches: PO Box 2001A, Berkeley, CA 94702, USA and London, UK

Printed by
Colorcraft Ltd, Hong Kong

Photographs by
Daniel Robinson (DR), Tony Wheeler (TW)

Front cover: Face Towers, the Bayon (TW)
Back cover: Mekong River, Phnom Penh (TW)

Published
September 1992

Although the authors and publisher have tried to make the information as accurate as possible, they accept no responsibility for any loss, injury or inconvenience sustained by any person using this book.

National Library of Australia Cataloguing in Publication Data

Robinson, Daniel
    Cambodia – a travel survival kit.

    1st ed.
    Includes index.
    ISBN 0 86442 174 5.

    1. Cambodia – Guidebooks. I. Title. (Series : Lonely Planet travel survival kit).

915.96044

text & maps © Lonely Planet 1992
photos © photographers as indicated 1992

All rights reserved. No part of this publication may be reproduced, stored in a retrieval system or transmitted in any form by any means, electronic, mechanical, photocopying, recording or otherwise, except brief extracts for the purpose of review, without the written permission of the publisher and copyright owner.

Daniel Robinson

Daniel was raised in the USA and Israel. He graduated from Princeton University with a BA in Near Eastern Studies. Daniel has travelled extensively in the Middle East and South, South-East and East Asia. He has also written a guide to Vietnam and chapters on France and Andorra for Lonely Planet.

Tony Wheeler

Tony Wheeler was born in England but spent most of his youth overseas. He returned to England to do a university degree in engineering, worked as an automative design engineer, returned to university to complete an MBA, then dropped out on the Asian overland trail with his wife Maureen. They've been travelling, writing and publishing guidebooks ever since, having set up Lonely Planet Publications in the mid-70s. Travel for the Wheelers is now considerably enlivened by their daughter Tashi and their son Kieran.

From the Authors

From Daniel I am greatly indebted to Mme Tan Sotho of the General Directorate of Tourism in Phnom Penh, who went well beyond the call of duty to make researching the Cambodia section possible despite very difficult conditions. I wish her and her daughter well. I would also like to thank So Hoan, his intrepid guide from Angkor Conservation; Gail Morrison of Australia, who is putting Cambodia's National Library back together; Claire Bel of Operation Handicap International; Mme Pan Chamnan of the General Directorate of Tourism; Chum Bun Rong, head of the Foreign Ministry's Press Department; Maya Krell of the Ecumenical Coalition on Third World Tourism; and his Phnom Penh cyclo driver, Sok San.

I would also like to acknowledge the assistance of Gloria Emerson of Princeton; Kevin Bowen, co-director of the William Joiner Center at U-Mass Boston; Judy Henchy, archivist of the Joiner Center; John McAuliffe of the US-Indochina Reconciliation Project in Philadelphia; Sarinah Kalb of Cambridge, Massachusetts; the Interlibrary

Loan Department and the Rare Books Collection staff of Firestone Library, Princeton University; Ross Meador and Carol Davis of Berkeley, CA; Jim Satterly of Atlanta; Drs Paul and Susan Balter of River Forest, IL; Alphonse Durieux of Guerneville, CA; Lisa Hsu of Princeton University; Son Nguyen & Tiffany Ho of New York; Thierry Di Costanzo of Avignon, France; Nevada Weir of Santa Fe, NM; Jill Kast Reuhrdanz of

Broomfield, CO; Professors Sadiq al-Azm, Charles Issawi, Mark Cohen and Andras Hamori and Dean Richard Williams of Princeton University.

Researching and writing this book would have been impossible without the encouragement and support of my parents - and their letting me take over half the house while writing this book. Thanks Mom. Thanks Dad.

For letters, thanks to: Patrick Field, Lorne Goldman (Canada), Paul Greening Jane Hinds (NZ), Brendon Hyde (Aust), Andy McNeilly (Aust) and Paul Stebbings (UK).

From Tony Thanks to Paul Cummings of Orbitours for organising the trip Maureen and I made to Cambodia at such short notice. Thanks also to our enthusiastic and helpful guides in Phnom Penh and Angkor.

This Edition

This new Cambodia book is essentially a revised version of the Cambodia chapters from *Vietnam, Laos & Cambodia - a travel survival kit.* Daniel Robinson researched and wrote this material but when Tony Wheeler visited Cambodia in 1992 it was obvious that the flow of visitors was growing so rapidly and the tourist infrastructure changing so fast that a book purely on Cambodia was justifiable.

From the Publisher

This edition of Cambodia was edited by Adrienne Costanzo and proofed by Diana Saad. Glenn Beanland was responsible for the mapping, design and cover design. Trudi Canavan and Vicki Beale provided additional mapping. Sue Mitra and Vicki took care of the production of the book.

Warning & Request

Things change, prices go up, schedules change, good places go bad and bad ones go bankrupt – nothing stays the same. So if you find things better or worse, recently opened or long since closed, please write and tell us and help make the next edition better!

Your letters will be used to help update future editions and, where possible, important changes will also be included as a Stop Press section in reprints.

All information is greatly appreciated, and the best letters will receive a free copy of the next edition, or any other Lonely Planet book of your choice.

Contents

Map Legend

BOUNDARIES

— ·· — ·· — ·· —	International Boundary
— ·· — ·· —	Internal Boundary
+·+·+·+·+·+·+·+	National Park or Reserve
— — — — — —	The Equator
··················	The Tropics

SYMBOLS

◉	NEW DELHI	National Capital
●	BOMBAY	Provincial or State Capital
●	Pune	Major Town
•	Barsi	Minor Town
■		Places to Stay
▼		Places to Eat
⬒		Post Office
✈		Airport
i		Tourist Information
⊖		Bus Station or Terminal
66		Highway Route Number
☪ ✝ ✟		Mosque, Church, Cathedral
∴		Temple or Ruin
✚		Hospital
※		Lookout
▲		Camping Area
⊓		Picnic Area
⌂		Hut or Chalet
▲		Mountain or Hill
		Railway Station
		Road Bridge
		Railway Bridge
		Road Tunnel
		Railway Tunnel
		Escarpment or Cliff
		Pass
		Ancient or Historic Wall

ROUTES

————	Major Road or Highway
- - - - - -	Unsealed Major Road
————	Sealed Road
- - - - - -	Unsealed Road or Track
═══════	City Street
+++++++++++	Railway
●━━◉━━●	Subway
··················	Walking Track
- - - - - -	Ferry Route
+I+I+I+I+I+I+	Cable Car or Chair Lift

HYDROGRAPHIC FEATURES

	River or Creek
	Intermittent Stream
	Lake, Intermittent Lake
	Coast Line
	Spring
	Waterfall
	Swamp
	Salt Lake or Reef
	Glacier

OTHER FEATURES

	Park, Garden or National Park
	Built Up Area
	Market or Pedestrian Mall
	Plaza or Town Square
	Cemetery

Note: not all symbols displayed above appear in this book

Introduction

Modern-day Cambodia is the successor-state of the mighty Khmer Empire, which during the Angkorian period (9th to 14th centuries) ruled much of what is now Vietnam, Laos and Thailand. The highly advanced, Indianised Khmer civilisation had an enormous influence on the cultural and artistic development of the other peoples of mainland South-East Asia. The magnificent temples of Angkor – of which Angkor Wat is the most famous – and over 1000 other monuments have long attracted pilgrims and tourists and are rapidly regaining their former popularity. Cambodia is just beginning to emerge from two decades of continual warfare and violence, including almost four years (1975-79) of rule by the genocidal Khmer Rouge, who killed at least

one million of Cambodia's seven million people. Even today, all around the country you see mass graves and ruined structures; the latter are the result not of neglect but of a conscious, coordinated campaign by the Khmer Rouge to smash the country's pre-revolutionary culture. And you see underpopulated towns and cities whose inhabitants are only slowly emerging from a nightmare that claimed the lives of their parents, spouses, siblings and children.

Although the Cambodian civil war is still smouldering, there is great hope that the huge UN force moving into the country will be able to restore peace and stability. As the country struggles to rebuild itself, the rest of the world is once again being allowed to visit Cambodia.

Among the brilliant achievements of Khmer civilisation that are open to foreign visitors for the first time in two decades are the fabled temples of Angkor, one of humanity's most magnificent architectural achievements. These stunning monuments, surrounded by dense jungle, are only 150 km from the Thai border, which is expected to open to tourist traffic as soon as the fighting is definitely over.

Other uniquely Cambodian sights include the plains and rice paddies of the country's heartland – dotted with sugar palms and peasants' thatch huts – which stretch off into the distance from the Tonlé Sap Lake and the Mekong River. In the south are the thickly forested Cardamom Mountains and Elephant Mountains; nearby are 354 km of coastline, much of it lined with unspoiled beaches. There are more mountains, as well as high plateaus, in the north-eastern provinces of Ratanakiri and Mondulkiri, many of whose inhabitants belong to the highland hill tribes.

The people of Cambodia seem a bit stunned by their country's recent history but are warmly welcoming towards Western visitors, whose very presence signifies that things are finally getting better for Cambodia. Hinayana Buddhist monks are proud to show you their rebuilt pagodas. And older people schooled long ago in English or French are eager to try out their rusty language skills on Westerners; so are young people diligently studying at private language schools along Phnom Penh's 'English St'. Accommodation and transport in Cambodia are still very basic, but for the adventurous traveller the country's delights more than compensate for the minor inconveniences.

Facts about the Country

What to Call Cambodia

Khmers have called their country Kampuchea (usually rendered Kambuja) since at least the 16th century. The name is derived from the word *kambu-ja*, meaning 'those born of Kambu' (a figure of Indian mythology), which was first used to refer to the people of Cambodia in the 10th century. The Portuguese 'Camboxa' and the French 'Cambodge', from which the English name 'Cambodia' is derived, are adaptations of 'Kambuja'.

Since gaining independence in 1953, the country has been known in English as:

1) The Kingdom of Cambodia (in French, le Royaume du Cambodge).
2) The Khmer Republic (under Lon Nol, who ruled from 1970 to 1975).
3) Democratic Kampuchea (under the Khmer Rouge, the Communist Party which controlled the country from 1975 to 1979).
4) The People's Republic of Kampuchea (under the Vietnamese- backed Phnom Penh government from 1979 to 1989).
5) The State of Cambodia (in French, L'État du Cambodge; in Khmer, Roët Kampuchea) from mid-1989.

It was the Khmer Rouge who insisted that the outside world use the name Kampuchea. Changing the country's official English name back to Cambodia (which has been used by the US State Department all along) was intended as a symbolic move to distance the present government in Phnom Penh from the bitter connotations of the name Kampuchea, which Westerners and overseas Khmer alike associate with the murderous Khmer Rouge regime.

HISTORY

Funan

From the 1st to the 6th centuries, much of present-day Cambodia was part of the kingdom of Funan, which owed its prosperity to its position on the great trade route between China and India; Funan's major port was Oc-Eo in what is now Kien Giang Province of southern Vietnam.

Funan (the name is a Chinese transliteration of the ancient Khmer form of the word *phnom*, which means 'hill') played a vitally important role in South-East Asian history as a recipient of Indian culture, which shaped the political institutions, culture and art of later Khmer states. Both Hinduism and Mahayana Buddhism coexisted within Funanese society. Princely links between Funan and the Khmers had been established by the 6th century, and subsequent Khmer dynasties viewed Funan as the state from which they sprang.

Chenla

In the middle of the 6th century, the Kambujas, who lived in the middle Mekong (north of present-day Cambodia), broke away from Funan. Within a short time, this new power, known as Chenla, absorbed the Funanese kingdom. In the late 7th century, Chenla broke into two divisions, called Land Chenla (to the north) and Water Chenla (to the south along the Gulf of Thailand) by the Chinese. Whereas Land Chenla was fairly stable during the 8th century, Water Chenla was beset by dynastic rivalries. During this period, Java probably invaded and controlled part of the country.

The Angkorian Period

The Angkorian period, known for its brilliant achievements in architecture and sculpture, was begun by Jayavarman II, a prince distantly related to earlier dynasties who returned from Java around the year 800. During his rule, a new state religion establishing the Khmer ruler as a god-king (*devaraja*) was instituted. Jayavarman II (reigned 802 to 850) installed himself successively at four different capitals around the

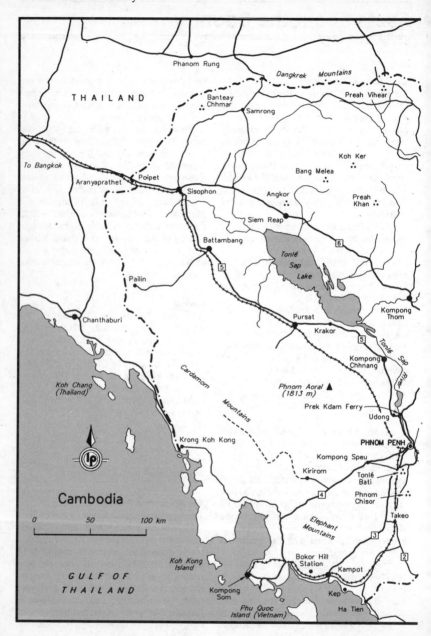

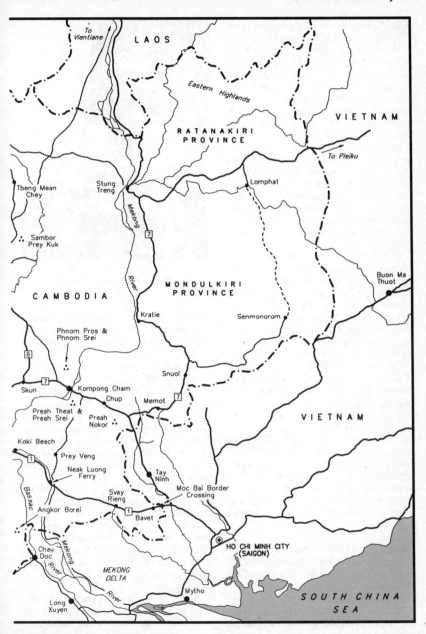

Tonlé Sap, the last of which was at Roluos, 13 km east of the modern town of Siem Reap.

Jayavarman II's nephew, Indravarman I (reigned 877 to 889), constructed a vast irrigation system that made possible the intensive cultivation of nearby lands. This and later irrigation projects allowed the Khmers to maintain a densely populated and highly centralised state in a relatively small area.

Indravarman I's successor, Yasovarman (reigned 889 to 910), moved the Khmer capital to the immediate vicinity of Angkor, where it would remain (except between 921 and 944 and during invasions) until the mid-15th century. Yasovarman and his immediate successors extended Khmer dominion over a vast area of what is now Vietnam, Laos and Thailand.

During the 11th and 12th centuries, the Khmers fought a series of wars with the Burmese, the Vietnamese and the Chams, whose empire was centred in south-central Vietnam. In the early 12th century, Champa was reduced to vassal status, but in 1177, the Chams avenged this humiliation by capturing and sacking the city of Angkor itself, leaving the Khmer Empire in chaos.

Order was restored by one of the greatest of all Khmer rulers, Jayavarman VII (reigned 1181 to 1201), who is best known for his huge building programme. Among the many monuments he constructed was his new capital, the massive city of Angkor Thom. Jayavarman VII pushed back the Chams and later laid waste to their kingdom, finally annexing Champa. But by the end of his reign, the Thais, who lived in the west of the empire, had begun to assert themselves.

For more information on the Angkorian period and its monuments, see the Angkor chapter.

Decline of the Khmer Empire

The decline of Angkor began after the death of Jayavarman VII at the beginning of the 13th century. During the course of the next 100 years, the Cambodian state abandoned its adherence to Hinduism, which had coexisted with Mahayana Buddhism since the 9th

Smiling Face, Angkor Thom

century, and embraced Hinayana Buddhism. The use of Sanskrit ended by the early 14th century; it was replaced as a sacred language by Pali.

During the 14th and 15th centuries, Khmer wealth and power were gradually eroded, in part because of repeated Thai incursions, which made maintaining the elaborate irrigation system on which Angkor's survival depended extremely difficult. In the mid-15th century, Angkor was occupied by the Thais, prompting the Khmer court to abandon the city and relocate their capital to the vicinity of Phnom Penh.

The next century and a half of Khmer history was dominated by confusing dynastic rivalries and almost continuous warfare with the Thais. Although the Khmers once pushed westward all the way to the Thai capital of Ayuthaya (only to find it occupied by the Burmese), the Thais recovered and dealt a crushing blow to the Khmers by capturing their capital in 1594.

Shortly before the Khmer defeat of 1594, the Cambodian king, Satha, requested the assistance of the Spanish and Portuguese, who had recently become active in the region. In 1596 a Spanish expedition arrived in Cambodia to assist Satha only to find that he had been deposed by a usurper, Chung Prei. After a series of disagreements and the sacking of the Chinese quarter of Phnom Penh by the Spanish forces, the Spanish attacked the palace and killed Chung Prei. The Spanish then decided to return to Manila, but while marching eastward through Laos, they changed their minds and returned to Phnom Penh, installing one of Satha's sons on the throne. Resentment of the power wielded by the Spanish grew among court officials until 1599, when the Spanish garrison at Phnom Penh was massacred. Shortly thereafter, Satha's brother ascended the throne with the help of the Thais.

From about 1600 until the arrival of the French in 1863, Cambodia was ruled by a series of weak kings who, because of continual challenges by dissident members of the royal family, were forced to seek the protection – granted, of course, at a price – of either Thailand or Vietnam. In the 17th century, assistance from the Nguyen Lords of southern Vietnam was given on the condition that Vietnamese be allowed to settle in what is now the southern region of Vietnam, at that time part of Cambodia, and today still referred to by the Khmers as 'Lower Cambodia'. In the west, the Thais established dominion over the provinces of Battambang and Siem Reap; by the late 18th century they had firm control of the Cambodian royal family. Indeed, one king was crowned in Bangkok and placed on the throne at Udong with the help of the Thai army. That Cambodia survived through the 18th century as a distinct entity is due to the preoccupations of its neighbours: while the Thais were expending their energy and resources in fighting the Burmese, the Vietnamese were wholly absorbed by internal strife, including the rivalry between the Trinh Lords and the Nguyen Lords and the Tay Son Rebellion.

French Rule

Cambodia's dual Thai and Vietnamese suzerainty ended in 1863, when French gunboats intimidated King Norodom (reigned 1860 to 1904) into signing a treaty of protectorate. French control of Cambodia, which developed as an adjunct to French colonial interests in Vietnam, at first involved relatively little direct interference in Cambodia's affairs of state. However, the French presence did prevent Cambodia's expansionist neighbours from annexing any more Khmer territory and helped keep Norodom on the throne despite the ambitions of his rebellious half-brothers.

By the 1870s, French officials in Cambodia began pressing for greater control over internal affairs. In 1884, Norodom was forced to sign a treaty turning his country into a virtual colony, sparking a two-year rebellion that constituted the only major anti-French movement in Cambodia until after WW II. This uprising ended when the king was persuaded to call upon rebel fighters to lay down their weapons in exchange for a return to the pretreaty arrangement.

During the next two decades, senior Cambodian officials, who saw certain advantages in acquiescing to French power, opened the door to direct French control over the day-to-day administration of the country. At the same time, the French maintained Norodom's court in a splendour probably unequalled since the Angkorian period, thereby greatly enhancing the symbolic position of the monarchy. The king's increased stature served to legitimise the Cambodian state, thereby pre-empting the growth of any sort of broad-based nationalist movement; this situation is in marked contrast to that of Vietnam. Indeed, the only large-scale popular protest of any kind between the 1880s and the 1940s was an essentially peaceful peasant uprising in 1916 which ended when the king agreed to consider their grievances.

King Norodom was succeeded by King Sisowath (reigned 1904 to 1927), who was followed on the throne by King Monivong (reigned 1927 to 1941). Upon King Monivong's death, the French governor general of Japanese-occupied Indochina,

Sihanouk

Admiral Jean Decoux, placed 18-year-old Prince Sihanouk on the Cambodian throne. The choice was based on the assumption that Sihanouk would prove pleasingly pliable; this proved to be a major miscalculation.

After WW II, the French returned, making Cambodia an 'autonomous state within the French Union' but retaining de facto control. The years after 1945 were marked by strife between the country's various political groupings, a situation made more unstable by the Franco-Vietminh War then raging in Vietnam and Laos.

Independence

In January 1953, King Sihanouk, who had been at odds with the dominant Democratic Party, took decisive action, dissolving the parliament, declaring martial law and embarking on what became known as the 'Royal Crusade': his campaign to drum up international support for his country's independence.

Independence was proclaimed on 9 November 1953 and recognised by the Geneva Conference of May 1954, which ended French control of Indochina. However, internal political turmoil continued, much of it the result of conflicts between Sihanouk and his domestic opponents. In March 1955, Sihanouk abdicated in favour of his father, Norodom Suramarit, in order to pursue a career as a politician. His newly established party, the People's Socialist Community (Sangkum Reastr Niyum), won every seat in parliament in the September 1955 elections. Sihanouk dominated Cambodian politics for the next 15 years, serving as prime minister until his father's death in 1960, when no new king was named and he became chief of state.

Although he also feared the Vietnamese Communists, during the early 1960s Sihanouk considered South Vietnam and Thailand, both allies of the USA (which he mistrusted), as the greatest threats to Cambodia's security and even survival. In an attempt to fend off these many dangers, he declared Cambodia neutral in international affairs. In May 1965, Sihanouk, convinced that the USA had been plotting against him and his family, broke diplomatic relations with Washington and tilted towards North Vietnam, the Viet Cong and China. In addition, he accepted that the North Vietnamese Army and the Viet Cong would use Cambodian territory in their battle against South Vietnam and the Americans.

These moves and his socialist economic policies alienated right-leaning elements in Cambodian society, including the officer corps of the army and the urban elite. At the same time, left-wing Cambodians, many of them educated abroad, deeply resented his internal policies, which did not allow for political dissent. Compounding Sihanouk's problems was the fact that all classes were fed up with the pervasive corruption. Although most peasants – the vast majority of the population – revered Sihanouk as a semi-divine figure, a rural-based rebellion broke out in 1967, leading him to conclude that the greatest threat to his regime now came from the left. Bowing to pressure from the army, he implemented a policy of harsh repression against left-wingers.

In 1969 the USA began a secret programme of bombing suspected communist base camps in Cambodia. For the next four years, until bombing was halted by the US Congress in August 1973, huge areas of the eastern half of the country were carpet bombed by US B-52s, killing uncounted thousands of civilians and turning hundreds of thousands more into refugees.

The Lon Nol Regime

By 1969 the conflict between the army and leftist rebels had become more serious and Sihanouk's political position had greatly deteriorated. In March 1970, while Sihanouk was on a trip to France, General Lon Nol and Prince Sisowath Matak, Sihanouk's cousin, deposed him as chief of state, apparently with US support. Pogroms against ethnic-Vietnamese living in Cambodia soon broke out, prompting many ethnic-Vietnamese inhabitants of the country to flee. Sihanouk took up residence in Beijing, where he set up a government-in-exile nominally in control of an indigenous Cambodian revolutionary movement that Sihanouk himself had nicknamed the Khmers Rouges (French for 'Red Khmers').

On 30 April 1970, US and South Vietnamese forces invaded Cambodia in an effort to rout out some 40,000 Viet Cong and North Vietnamese troops that were using bases inside Cambodia in their war to overthrow the South Vietnamese government. As a result of the invasion, the Vietnamese Communists withdrew deeper into Cambodia, thus posing an even greater threat to the Lon Nol government than before. At the same time, the new government was becoming very unpopular as a result of the unprecedented greed and corruption of its leaders. Savage fighting quickly engulfed the entire country, bringing misery to millions of Cambodians, many of whom fled rural areas for the relative safety of Phnom Penh and provincial capitals. Between 1970 and 1975, several hundred thousand people died in the fighting.

During the next few years, the Khmer Rouge came to play a dominant role in trying to overthrow the Lon Nol regime. The leaders of the Khmer Rouge, including Paris-educated Pol Pot (Saloth Sar) and Khieu Samphan, had fled into the countryside in the 1960s to escape the summary justice then being meted out to suspected leftists by Sihanouk's security forces.

Despite massive US military and economic aid, Lon Nol never succeeded in gaining the initiative against the Khmer Rouge, which pursued a strategy of attrition. Large parts of the countryside fell to the rebels, and many provincial capitals were cut off from Phnom Penh. On 17 April 1975 – two weeks before the fall of Saigon – Phnom Penh surrendered to the Khmer Rouge.

The Khmer Rouge Regime

Upon taking Phnom Penh, the Khmer Rouge implemented one of the most radical and brutal restructurings of a society ever attempted; its goal was to transform Cambodia into a Maoist, peasant-dominated agrarian cooperative. Within two weeks of coming to power, the entire populations of the capital and provincial towns, including everyone in the hospitals, were force-marched out to the countryside and placed in mobile work teams to do slave labour – preparing the fields, digging irrigation canals – for 12 to 15 hours a day. Disobedience of any sort often brought immediate execution. The advent of Khmer Rouge rule was proclaimed 'Year Zero'. Currency was abolished and postal services were halted. Except for one fortnightly flight to Beijing (China was providing aid and advisors to the Khmer Rouge), the country was completely cut off from the outside world.

Over the next four years, hundreds of thousands of Cambodians, including the vast majority of the country's educated people, were tortured to death or executed in what some have called a campaign of 'auto-genocide'. Thousands of middle-class Cambodians, branded as 'parasites' because they spoke a foreign language or wore spectacles, were systematically liquidated. The slaughter reached its height in 1978, when huge numbers of people accused of being traitors or Vietnamese spies were killed. Hundreds of thousands more died of mistreatment, malnourishment and disease. At least one million Cambodians died between 1975 and 1979 as a result of the policies of the Khmer Rouge government.

Sihanouk returned to Phnom Penh in September 1975 as titular chief of state but resigned three months later. He remained in Phnom Penh, imprisoned in his palace and was kept alive only at the insistence of the Chinese, who considered him useful. During the Vietnamese invasion of Cambodia in December 1978, Sihanouk was flown to Beijing to prevent his falling into the hands of the new government.

Vietnamese Intervention

Between 1976 and 1978, the xenophobic government in Phnom Penh instigated a series of border clashes with Vietnam, whose southern region – once part of the Khmer Empire – it claimed. Khmer Rouge incursions into Vietnamese border provinces left hundreds of Vietnamese civilians dead. On 25 December 1978, Vietnam launched a full-scale invasion of Cambodia, toppling the Pol Pot government two weeks later (on 7 January 1979). As Vietnamese tanks neared Phnom Penh, the Khmer Rouge fled westward with as many civilians as they could seize, taking refuge in the jungles and mountains on both sides of the border with Thailand. The Vietnamese installed a new government led by two former Khmer Rouge officers, Hun Sen, who had defected to Vietnam in 1977, and Heng Samrin, who had done the same in 1978. The official version of events is that the Heng Samrin government came to power in a revolutionary uprising against the Pol Pot regime.

The social and economic dislocation that accompanied the Vietnamese invasion – along with the destruction of rice stocks and unharvested fields by both sides (to prevent their use by the enemy) – resulted in a vastly reduced rice harvest in early 1979. The chaotic situation led to very little rice being planted in the summer of 1979. By the middle of that year, the country was on the verge of widespread famine. As hundreds of thousands of Cambodians fled to Thailand, a massive international famine relief effort, sponsored by the UN, was launched.

In June 1982, Sihanouk agreed, under pressure from China, to head a military and political front opposed to the Phnom Penh government and the 170,000 Vietnamese troops defending it. The Sihanouk-led resistance coalition brought together – on paper, at least – FUNCINPEC (the French acronym for Cambodian National Front for an Independent, Neutral, Peaceful and Cooperative Cambodia), which comprised a royalist group loyal to Sihanouk; the Khmer People's National Liberation Front, a non-Communist grouping formed by former prime minister and banker Son Sann; and the Khmer Rouge, officially known as the Party of Democratic Kampuchea and by far the largest and most powerful of the three. Despite Pol Pot's 'retirement' in 1985, he remains the de facto leader of the Khmer Rouge.

By the late 1980s, the weak royalist group, the Armée Nationale Sihanoukiste, had 12,000 troops; Son Sann's faction, plagued by internal divisions, could field some 8000 soldiers; and the Khmer Rouge's National Army of Democratic Kampuchea was believed to have 40,000 troops. The army of the Phnom Penh government, the Kampuchean People's Revolutionary Armed Forces, had 50,000 regular soldiers and another 100,000 men and women serving in local militia forces.

In 1985, the Vietnamese overran all the major rebel camps inside Cambodia, forcing the Khmer Rouge and their allies to retreat into Thailand. Since that time, the Khmer Rouge – and, to a much more limited extent, the other two factions – have engaged in guerrilla warfare aimed at demoralising their opponents. Tactics used by the Khmer Rouge include shelling government-controlled garrison towns, planting thousands of mines along roads and in rice fields, attacking road transport, blowing up bridges, kidnapping village chiefs and killing local administrators and school teachers. The Khmer Rouge has also forced thousands of men, women and children living in the refugee camps it controls to work as porters, ferrying ammunition and other supplies into Cambodia across heavily mined sections of the border.

Throughout the 1980s, Thailand actively supported the Khmer Rouge and the other resistance factions, seeing them as a counterweight to Vietnamese power in the region. In fact, in 1979 Thailand demanded that as a condition for allowing international food aid for Cambodia to pass through its territory, food had to be supplied to the Khmer Rouge forces encamped in the Thai border region as well. Along with weaponry supplied by China (and delivered by the Thai army), this international assistance was essential in enabling the Khmer Rouge to rebuild its military strength. At the same time, Malaysia and Singapore supplied weapons to the two smaller factions of the coalition. As part of its campaign to harass and isolate Hanoi (capital of Vietnam), the USA gave more than US$15 million a year in aid to the non-Communist factions of the Khmer Rouge-dominated coalition and helped it to retain its UN seat.

Cambodia Today

Although over a decade has passed since the overthrow of the Pol Pot government, the tragedy and trauma of its 57 murderous months in power still pervade every aspect of Cambodian social life and politics. And Pol Pot, accompanied by his new wife (his former wife is said to be insane and living in Beijing), still commands his Chinese-equipped forces from a heavily guarded compound just inside Thailand's Trat Province.

Most foreign observers in Cambodia believe that the Vietnamese-installed Phnom Penh government is accepted as legitimate by the vast majority of the Cambodian people, who resent the Vietnamese but appreciate their role in bringing down the genocidal Khmer Rouge regime and preventing its return to power. Sihanouk is remembered with nostalgia by a few older Cambodians, but his repressive policies before 1970 and his association with the

Khmer Rouge since then are the cause of great bitterness.

In September 1989 Vietnam, suffering from economic woes and eager to reduce its international isolation, announced that it had withdrawn all of its troops from Cambodia; however, evidence suggests that Vietnamese soldiers wearing Cambodian uniforms remained in the country well into 1990. With most of the Vietnamese gone, the opposition coalition, still dominated by the Khmer Rouge, launched a series of offensives, bringing the number of refugees inside the country to over 150,000 by the autumn of 1990. In the first eight months of 1990, over 2000 Cambodians lost their lives in the fighting.

Since the late 1980s, the Hun Sen government in Phnom Penh has made concerted efforts to gain international recognition – especially in the West – by working to change its image as a puppet of the Vietnamese. People who served in the Sihanouk and Lon Nol governments, many of whom were trained in Europe or the USA, have been given positions of power in the present government; such people now make up about half the cabinet. At the same time, socialist dogma has been discarded in favour of free-market economic principles, in evidence in the many private shops now operating in the capital and elsewhere. Some 70% of the economy is now in private hands, which is more than in the 1960s under Sihanouk. This process is being accelerated by the withdrawal of Soviet-bloc economic aid, which until recently accounted for 80% of government revenues. However, watchdog groups report that human rights violations are continuing. In 1989 and 1990, for example, the Phnom Penh government resorted to nighttime sweeps of discos and cinemas to fill the ranks of its army, dragging off young men and boys as young as 13 for immediate conscription.

In the late 1980s, the USA made a total Vietnamese withdrawal from Cambodia and Vietnamese cooperation in bringing about a comprehensive solution to the Cambodian civil war prerequisites for establishing diplomatic relations with Hanoi. In July 1990, in a major shift of US foreign policy, the USA initiated diplomatic contacts with Vietnam – the first between Washington and Hanoi since the late 1970s – to discuss the Cambodian situation. At the same time, the USA withdrew diplomatic support for the Khmer Rouge-dominated coalition and announced that it would, at the next General Assembly session, oppose seating the coalition's UN delegation. A few months later, the USA began its first-ever diplomatic contacts with the Phnom Penh government; shortly thereafter, China did the same.

Diplomatic efforts to end the civil war began to bear fruit in September 1990, when a plan agreed upon by the five permanent members of the UN Security Council (the USA, the former USSR, China, France and Britain) was accepted by both the Phnom Penh government and the three factions of the resistance coalition.

According to the agreement, a largely symbolic Supreme National Council, comprised of six individuals selected by the Phnom Penh government and an equal number chosen by the opposition (two from each faction), would be constituted under the leadership of Sihanouk. The Council, considered the embodiment of Cambodian sovereignty, would then cede its authority in the key areas of foreign affairs, defence, internal security, finance and information to a UN-run transition government, which would disarm rebel factions and administer free and fair elections. The plan, costing between US$3 and US$5 billion and requiring up to 20,000 officials and troops, is the most ambitious such mission ever taken by the United Nations.

After months of bickering the agreement was finally hammered out at the Paris Accord of 23 October 1991, and on 14 November Sihanouk returned to Cambodia. Sihanouk was welcomed with open arms but when Khmer Rouge leader Khieu Samphan turned up two weeks later he was met by an angry mob who tried to lynch him. The shaken Khieu Samphan scuttled back quickly to Bangkok to rethink the situation.

A small force of troops from UNAMIC, the United Nations Advance Mission to Cambodia, led by an Australian contingent, was in place late in 1991 but it is supposed to be only the forerunner of a much larger contingent from UNTAC, the United Nations Transitional Authority in Cambodia. Their first forces started to arrive in early '92 but getting UNTAC in place was proving to be a formidable problem, hampered by other distractions like the civil war in Yugoslavia. If the required 'neutral political environment' can be produced, then elections will be held in April 1993.

The UN task will be a difficult one. The warring factions have to be disarmed and demobilised before the refugees from the Thai border area can be moved back into the country. City corruption is a major problem and could easily recreate the divisions between greedy urban areas and impoverished rural areas which led to the growth of the Khmer Rouge in the first place. On the other hand the bustling markets, the rapid resurgence of tourism to Angkor and the activities of aid organisations like the Halo Trust, which is attempting to map the Cambodian minefields, gives some hope for a brighter future.

GEOGRAPHY

Cambodia covers a land area of 181,035 sq km, which is the size of Missouri and a bit over half the size of Italy or Vietnam. The country's maximum extent is about 580 km from east to west and 450 km from north to south. Cambodia is bounded on the west by Thailand, on the north by Thailand and Laos, on the east and south-east by Vietnam and on the south by the Gulf of Thailand.

Cambodia's two dominant topographical features are the Mekong River, which is almost five km wide in places, and the Tonlé Sap (Great Lake). The Mekong, which rises in Tibet, flows about 315 km through Cambodia before continuing on, via southern Vietnam, to the South China Sea. At Phnom Penh, it splits into its two major branches: the Upper River (called simply the Mekong or, in Vietnamese, the Tien Giang) and the

Lower River (the Bassac River; in Vietnamese, the Hau Giang). The rich sediment deposited during the Mekong's annual wet-season flooding has made for very fertile agricultural land. Most of Cambodia's streams and rivers flow into the Mekong-Tonlé Sap basin.

The Tonlé Sap is linked to the Mekong at Phnom Penh by a 100 km long channel which I have called, for convenience' sake, the Tonlé Sap River. From mid-May to early October (the rainy season), the level of the Mekong rises, backing up the Tonlé Sap River and causing it to flow north-westward into the Tonlé Sap Lake. During this period, the Tonlé Sap swells from 3000 sq km to over 7500 sq km; its maximum depth increases from about 2.2 metres to more than 10 metres. As the water level of the Mekong falls during the dry season, the Tonlé Sap River reverses its flow, draining the waters of the lake back into the Mekong. This extraordinary process makes the Tonlé Sap one of the world's richest sources of fresh-water fish.

In the centre of Cambodia, around the Tonlé Sap and the upper Mekong Delta, is a low-lying alluvial plain where the vast majority of Cambodia's people live. Extending outward from this plain are thinly forested transitional plains with elevations of no more than about 100 metres above sea level.

In the south-west, much of the area between the Gulf of Thailand and the Tonlé Sap is covered by a highland region formed by two distinct upland blocks: the Cardamom Mountains (Chuor Phnom Kravanh) in south-western Battambang Province and Pursat Province, and the Elephant Mountains (Chuor Phnom Damrei) in the provinces of Kompong Speu, Koh Kong and Kampot. Along the southern coast is a heavily forested lowland strip isolated from the rest of the country by the mountains to the north. Cambodia's highest peak, Phnom Aoral (1813 metres), is on the eastern part of the border, between the provinces of Kompong Chhnang and Kompong Speu.

Along Cambodia's northern border with Thailand, the plains abut an east-west oriented sandstone escarpment, over 300 km long and 180 to 550 metres in height, that marks the southern limit of the Dangkrek Mountains (Chuor Phnom Dangkrek). In the north-eastern corner of the country (the provinces of Ratanakiri and Mondulkiri), the transitional plains give way to the Eastern Highlands, a remote region of densely forested mountains and high plateaus that extends eastward into Vietnam's Central Highlands and northward into Laos.

CLIMATE

The climate of Cambodia is governed by two monsoons, which set the rhythm of rural life. The cool, dry, north-eastern monsoon, which carries little rain, blows from about November to March. From May to early October, the south-western monsoon brings strong winds, high humidity and heavy rains. Between these seasons, the weather is transitional. Even during the wet season, it rarely rains in the morning: most precipitation comes in the afternoons, and even then only sporadically.

Maximum daily temperatures range from 35°C in April, the hottest month, to the high 20s during January, the coolest month. Daily minimum temperatures are usually about 8°C to 11°C below the maximums.

Annual rainfall varies considerably from area to area. Whereas the seaward slopes of the south-western highlands receive more than 5000 mm of precipitation per annum, the central lowlands average only about 1400 mm. Between 70% and 80% of the annual rainfall is brought by the south-western monsoon.

FLORA

The central lowland consists of rice paddies, fields of dry crops such as corn and tobacco, tracts of reeds and tall grass, and thinly wooded areas. The transitional plains are mostly covered with savanna grasses, which grow to a height of 1.5 metres.

In the south-west, there are virgin rainforests growing to heights of 50 metres or more on the rainy seaward slopes of the mountains, while, nearby, higher elevations support pine forests. Vegetation in the coastal strip includes both evergreen and mangrove forests. In the northern mountains there are broadleaf evergreen forests with trees soaring 30 metres above the thick undergrowth of vines, bamboos, palms and assorted woody and herbaceous ground plants. The Eastern Highlands are covered with grassland and deciduous forest. Forested upland areas support many varieties of orchid.

In the last two decades, a great deal of deforestation has taken place, in part because firewood remains Cambodia's principal source of energy. In the north-east, a large quantity of timber is being cut by the Vietnamese.

The symbol of Cambodia is the sugar palm tree, which is used in construction (for roofs and walls) and to make medicine, wine and vinegar. Because of the way sugar palms grow (over the years, the tree keeps getting taller but the trunk, which lacks a normal bark, does not grow thicker), their trunks retain shrapnel marks from every battle that ever raged around them. Some sugar palms survive despite having been shot clear through the trunk.

FAUNA

Cambodia's larger wild animals include bears, elephants, rhinoceros, leopards, tigers and wild oxen. The lion, although often incorporated into Angkorian heraldic devices, has never been seen here. Among the country's more common birds are cormorants, cranes, egrets, grouse, herons, pelicans, pheasants and wild ducks. There is also a great variety of butterflies. Four types of snake are especially dangerous: the cobra, the king cobra, the banded krait and Russell's viper.

GOVERNMENT

Most of the territory of Cambodia is under the control of the government that was installed in Phnom Penh by the Vietnamese after their overthrow of the Khmer Rouge in 1979. That government is led by two former Khmer Rouge officers: Prime Minister Hun Sen, a widely respected reformer, and President of the Council of State Heng Samrin, who is known as a hardliner. Heng Samrin is also Secretary General of the ruling party, the People's Revolutionary Party, which has about 10,000 members. The highest legislative body is the National Assembly, which has 117 members. The highest executive body is the Council of State.

The flag of the Phnom Penh government is a yellow, five-tower outline of Angkor in the middle of a blue-and-red field split horizontally. This flag replaced one consisting of a yellow, five-tower outline of Angkor on an all-red field in 1989. The flag of the Khmer Rouge-dominated coalition nominally led by Prince Sihanouk had a yellow, three-tower outline of Angkor on a red field.

Cambodia is divided into 18 provinces *(khet)*, 122 districts *(srok)*, 1570 sub-districts *(khum)* and 11,564 villages *(phoum)*. Below the village levels are sub-divisions known as 'solidarity groups' *(krom samaki)*, each consisting of about 15 families organised on a cooperative or collective basis. Cambodia's provinces, listed from east to west, are: Ratanakiri, Mondulkiri, Stung Treng, Kompong Cham, Kratie, Svay Rieng, Prey Veng, Preah Vihear, Kompong Thom, Kandal, Takeo, Kompong Chhnang, Kompong Speu, Kampot, Siem Reap-Oddar Meanchey, Pursat, Koh Kong and Battambang. Most of Cambodia's provinces bear the same name as their capital city.

ECONOMY

Cambodia's economy, which even before 1975 was one of the least developed in South-East Asia, is based on two major products, rice and rubber, both of which are subject to the vagaries of the weather and large fluctuations in world market prices. Other important products include fish (the single most important source of protein in the Cambodian diet), livestock, fruits (especially bananas, oranges and pineapples), garden vegetables, beans, cassava, corn (maize), sugar, soya beans, sweet potatoes, tobacco, coffee and kapok (silky fibres that clothe the seed of the ceiba tree and are used as a filling for mattresses and similar items). During the 1980s, domestic agricultural production was supplemented by food aid from Vietnam and the USSR.

About 80% of the population is employed in agriculture, fishing or forestry. Until the dislocations of the early 1970s, approximately four-fifths of the country's farmers owned the land they farmed; most plots were quite small (one hectare or less). Rice, which provided over one-third of the gross national product, was grown by 80% of rural families on some 85% of the country's total cultivated land area. Most regions produced only one crop a year because of a lack of irrigation infrastructure. Peasants supplemented their subsistence-level rice crop by raising livestock, cultivating fruit and vegetables and fishing for carp, lungfish, perch, smelt and other varieties of freshwater fish.

All fuel and most raw materials, equipment and consumer goods must be imported. Cambodia's main trading partners are Vietnam (which of late has been doing a lot of hardwood logging in the north-east), the former Soviet Union, Eastern Europe and, through extensive smuggling networks, Thailand and Singapore. Precious stones mined around Pailin and elsewhere in Battambang Province – these days controlled by the Khmer Rouge – are exported across the border to Thailand.

Recently, plans to enact a foreign investment law similar to those promulgated in Vietnam and Laos in the late 1980s have been drawn up, and Singapore, Thailand and Australia have been showing interest in expanding their economic contacts with Cambodia.

POPULATION

In the late 1980s, the population of Cambodia was somewhere around seven million, with city and town-dwellers making up about 10% of the total. In the central lowlands, where 90% of Cambodians reside, the population density is 100 people per sq km; by comparison, Vietnam's Red River Delta has 1000 people per sq km. The average national population density is only 37 people per sq km.

The country's rate of population growth is now estimated to be over 3% per annum, among the highest in the world. Birth rates are said to be especially high in the refugee camps along the Thai border. During the Vietnamese occupation there was a substantial inflow of Vietnamese settlers which some estimate at over one million.

PEOPLE
Ethnic-Khmers

Between 90% and 95% of the people who live in Cambodia are ethnic-Khmers (ethnic-Cambodians), making the country the most homogeneous in South-East Asia.

The Khmers have inhabited Cambodia since the beginning of recorded history (around the 2nd century AD), many centuries before the Thais and Vietnamese migrated to the region. During the next six centuries, Khmer culture and religion were Indianised by contact with the civilisations of India and Java. Over the centuries, the Khmers have mixed with other groups resident in Cambodia, including the Javanese (8th century), Thai (10th to 15th centuries), Vietnamese (from the early 17th century) and Chinese (since the 18th century).

Ethnic-Chinese

The most important minority group in Cambodia is the Chinese, who until 1975 controlled the country's economic life. Although intermarriage with the Khmers is not infrequent, the Chinese have managed to retain a significant degree of cultural distinctiveness. In 1975, some 250,000 ethnic-Chinese resided in Cambodia, but like other city dwellers, they suffered especially severely under the Khmer Rouge. Their numbers have been further reduced by the disproportionate number of ethnic-Chinese who have chosen to emigrate since 1979.

Ethnic-Vietnamese

There is a great deal of mutual dislike and distrust between the Cambodians and the

Vietnamese, even those who have been living in Cambodia for generations. While the Khmers refer to the Vietnamese as *yuon*, a derogatory term that means 'barbarians', the Vietnamese look down on the Khmers and consider them lazy for not farming every available bit of land, an absolute necessity in densely populated Vietnam. Historic antagonisms between the Vietnamese and the Khmers are exacerbated by the prominence of ethnic-Vietnamese among shopowners.

Before 1970, Cambodia had between 250,000 and 300,000 ethnic-Vietnamese, a large number of whom lived by fishing in the Tonlé Sap. Significant numbers of them fled during the reign of anti-Vietnamese terror unleashed by the Lon Nol government. After 1979, many of these refugees returned to Cambodia, joined, some observers charge, by hundreds of thousands of settlers sent in by Hanoi to colonise the country. Today, ethnic-Vietnamese are again fleeing to Vietnam, preferring, as one Cambodian put it, to return to Vietnam alive rather than floating down the Mekong dead, as did some of their less fortunate compatriots in the early 1970s.

Cham Muslims

Cambodia's Cham Muslims (known locally as the Khmer Islam) currently number some 190,000. They live in 200 villages, mostly in areas along the Mekong to the north and east of Phnom Penh. The Cham Muslims suffered particularly vicious persecution between 1975 and 1979 when a large part of their community was exterminated. Of the country's 113 mosques in 1975, only 20 have been rebuilt and reconsecrated.

Ethno-Linguistic Minorities

Cambodia's diverse ethno-linguistic minorities (hill tribes), who live in the country's mountainous regions, numbered approximately 90,000 in 1975. Collectively, they are known to Khmers by the derogatory term *phnong*, which means 'savages'.

These groups, which include the Saoch (in the Elephant Mountains), the Pear (in the Cardamom Mountains), the Brao (along the Lao border) and the Kuy (in the far north-west), have been mistreated by the ethnic-Khmers for centuries, although they were spared the worst excesses of the Khmer Rouge.

EDUCATION

In 1970, it was estimated that about 50% of the population aged 10 and over could read, the lowest rate in South-East Asia except for Laos.

ARTS

Between the 15th century, when Angkor fell to the Thais and was abandoned, and the advent of the French protectorate in 1863, foreign invasions, civil war, depopulation and general political instability left little opportunity and few resources to keep Cambodia's artistic traditions alive. In recent generations, Cambodia's consciousness of the glory of its past achievements has tended to dominate artistic expression, leading to conservatism rather than innovation in the arts.

Architecture

Khmer architecture reached its period of greatest magnificence during the Angkorian era (the 9th to 14th centuries). Some of the finest examples of architecture from this period are Angkor Wat and the structures of Angkor Thom.

Today, most Cambodian houses in rural areas are built on high wood pilings (if the family can afford it) and have thatch roofs, walls made of palm mats and floors of woven bamboo strips resting on bamboo joists. The shady space underneath is used for storage and for people to relax at midday.

Sculpture

Many of the finest works of Khmer sculpture are on display at the National Museum in Phnom Penh.

Music, Dance & Theatre

Cambodia's highly stylised classic dance, adapted from dances performed at Angkor (and similar to Thai dances derived from the same source), is performed to the accompaniment of an orchestra and choral narration. The dancers act out stories and legends taken from Hindu epics such as the *Ramayana.*

In the countryside, wandering troupes perform folk dramas and folk dances at festivals and weddings. The actors invariably depict stereotyped characters familiar to the audience: the beautiful princess, the greedy merchant, the inept lover, the cruel father, the country bumpkin and so forth.

About 90% of Cambodia's classical dancers were killed by the Khmer Rouge. The government has recently re-established a national classical dance troupe.

CULTURE
Greetings
Cambodians traditionally greet each other by pressing their hands together in front of their bodies and bowing. In recent decades, this custom has been partially replaced by the Western practice of shaking hands. But, although men tend to shake hands with each other, women usually use the traditional greeting with both men and women. It is considered acceptable (or perhaps excusable) for foreigners to shake hands with Cambodians of both sexes.

Dress
Both men and women often wear sarongs (made of cotton, a cotton-synthetic blend or silk), especially at home. Men who can afford it usually prefer silk sarongs. Under Lon Nol (ruled 1970 to 1975), it was forbidden to wear sarongs in public because, as one Cambodian explained to me, the government considered the sarong to be as unfit for use outside the home as pyjamas would be in the West.

On formal occasions such as religious festivals and family celebrations, women often wear *hols* during the daytime. At night, they change into single-colour silk garments called *phamuongs*, which are decorated along the hems.

Modesty
The women of Cambodia are very modest in their dress – much more so than the Vietnamese. When eating at home, they sit on floor mats with their feet to the side rather than in the lotus position, as do the men. As in Thailand, nude bathing is unacceptable in Cambodia.

Visiting Pagodas
The Khmer are a tolerant people and may choose not to point out improper behaviour to their foreign guests, but you should dress and act with the utmost respect when visiting wats or other religious sites (such as some of the temples of Angkor). This is all the more important given the vital role Buddhist beliefs and institutions have played in the lives of many Cambodians in the aftermath of the Khmer Rouge holocaust. Proper etiquette in pagodas is mostly a matter of common sense. A few tips:

1) Don't wear shorts or tank tops.
2) Take off your hat when entering the grounds of the wat.
3) Take off your shoes before going into the *vihara* (sanctuary).
4) If you sit down in front of the dais (the platform on which the Buddhas are placed), sit with your feet to the side rather than in the lotus position.
5) Never point your finger – or, heaven forbid, the soles of your feet – towards a figure of the Buddha or human beings either.

Addressing People
Members of the family or people whom you wish to treat as friends should be addressed according to the following rules:

1) People of your age or younger can be called by name.
2) People older than yourself should be addressed as *Bang* (for men) or *Bang Srey* (for women).
3) Elderly people should be addressed as *Ta* (for men) and *Yeay* (for women).

Officials and informal acquaintances are officially supposed to be addressed by usages approximating 'comrade', but in practice people use *Lok* (Mr) and *Lok Srey* (Mrs), which convey respect coupled with a bit of formality and distance. When speaking with such people in English, it is probably best to use 'Mr' and 'Mrs'.

Miscellaneous

The following are a few general tips about proper behaviour in Cambodia:

1) Getting angry and showing it by shouting or becoming abusive is both impolite and a poor reflection on you; in addition, it is unlikely to accomplish much. If things aren't being done as they should, remember that there is a critical shortage of trained people in the country because the vast majority of educated Cambodians either fled the country or were killed between 1975 and 1979.

2) As in Thailand, it is improper to pat children on the head.

3) If you would like someone to come over to you, motion with your whole hand held palm down – signalling with your index finger and your palm pointed skyward may be interpreted as being sexually suggestive.

4) When picking your teeth with a toothpick after a meal, it is considered polite to hold the toothpick in one hand and to cover your open mouth with the other.

5) Everyone wears thongs or flip-flops (rubber sandals; in Khmer, *sbek choeung phtoat*), even civil servants, though such footwear was once considered appropriate only at home. Among revolutionaries, thongs used to be worn in order to demonstrate one's detachment from the material world, but these days they remain popular because few people can afford anything else.

RELIGION
Hinduism

Hinduism flourished alongside Buddhism from the 1st century until the 14th century. In Funan and during the pre-Angkorian period, Hinduism was represented by the worship of Harihara (Shiva and Vishnu embodied in a single deity). During the time of Angkor, Shiva was the deity most in favour with the royal family, although in the 12th century he seems to have been superseded by Vishnu.

Buddhism

The majority of the people of Cambodia are followers of Theravada, or Hinayana, Buddhism. Buddhism was introduced to Cambodia between the 13th and 14th centuries and was the state religion until 1975.

The Theravada (Teaching of the Elders) school of Buddhism is an earlier and, according to its followers, less corrupted form of Buddhism than the Mahayana schools found in East Asia or in the Himalayan lands. The Theravada school is also called the 'Southern' school since it took the southern route from India, its place of origin, through South-East Asia (Myanmar/Burma, Thailand, Laos and Cambodia in this case), while the 'Northern' school proceeded north into Nepal, Tibet, China, Korea, Mongolia, Vietnam and Japan. Because the southern school tried to preserve or limit the Buddhist doctrines to only those canons codified in the early Buddhist era, the northern school gave Theravada Buddhism the name Hinayana, meaning the 'Lesser Vehicle'. They considered themselves Mahayana, the 'Great Vehicle', because they built upon the earlier teachings, 'expanding' the doctrine to respond more to the needs of lay people, or so it is claimed.

Theravada, or Hinayana, doctrine stresses the three principal aspects of existence; *dukkha* (suffering, unsatisfactoriness, disease), *anicca* (impermanency, transience of all things) and *anatta* (non-substantiality or non-essentiality of reality: no permanent 'soul'). These concepts, when 'discovered' by Siddhartha Gautama in the 6th century BC, were in direct contrast to the Hindu belief in an eternal, blissful Self, or *Paramatman*, hence Buddhism was originally a 'heresy' against India's Brahmanic religion.

Gautama, an Indian prince-turned-ascetic, subjected himself to many years of severe austerities to arrive at this vision of the world and was given the title Buddha, 'the Enlightened' or 'the Awakened'. Gautama

Buddha spoke of four noble truths which had the power to liberate any human being who could realise them. These four noble truths are:

1) The truth of suffering – 'Existence is suffering'.
2) The truth of the cause of suffering – 'Suffering is caused by desire'.
3) The truth of the cessation of suffering – 'Eliminate the cause of suffering (desire) and suffering will cease to arise'.
4) The truth of the path – 'The eight-fold path is the way to eliminate desire/extinguish suffering'.

The eight-fold path (*atthangika-magga*) consists of: (1) right understanding; (2) right-mindedness (or 'right thought'); (3) right speech; (4) right bodily conduct; (5) right livelihood; (6) right effort; (7) right attentiveness; and (8) right concentration. These eight limbs belong to three different 'pillars' of practice: morality, or *sila* (3-5); concentration, or *samadhi* (7 & 8); and wisdom, or *panna* (1 & 2). Some Buddhists believe the path, called the Middle Way since ideally it avoids both extreme austerity as well as extreme sensuality, is to be taken in successive stages, while others say the pillars are interdependent.

The ultimate goal of Theravada Buddhism is *nibbana* (Sanskrit: nirvana) which literally means the 'blowing-out' or 'extinction' of all causes of *dukkha*. Effectively it means an end to all corporeal existence – an end to that which is forever subject to suffering and which is conditioned from moment to moment by *karma*, or action. In reality, most Buddhists aim for rebirth in a 'better' existence rather than the supramundane goal of *nibbana*, which is highly misunderstood by Asians as well as Westerners. Many Buddhists express the feeling that they are somehow unworthy of nibbana. By feeding monks, giving donations to temples and performing regular worship at the local wat (Thai Buddhist temple) they hope to improve their lot, acquiring enough merit (Pali: *punña*) to prevent or at least lessen the number of rebirths. The making of merit is an important social as well as religious activity. The concept of reincarnation is almost universally accepted by Cambodian Buddhists, and to some extent even by non-Buddhists.

The *Trilatna* (*triratna*), or Triple Gems, include the Buddha, the Dhamma (the teachings) and the Sangha (the Buddhist brotherhood). The Buddha in his sculptural form is found on high shelves or altars in homes and shops as well as in temples. The Dhamma is chanted morning and evening in every wat. The Sangha is represented by the street presence of orange-robed monks, especially in the early morning hours when they perform their alms-rounds, in what has almost become a travel-guide cliche in motion.

Socially, every Buddhist male is expected to become a monk for a short period in his life, optimally between the time he finishes school and starts a career or marries. Men or boys under 20 years of age may enter the Sangha as novices and this is not unusual since a family earns great merit when one of its sons takes robe and bowl. Traditionally, the length of time spent in the wat is three months, during the Buddhist Lent (*phansaa* or *watsa*), which begins in July and coincides with the rainy season. However, nowadays men may spend as little as a week or 15 days to accrue merit as monks.

Monks must follow 227 vows or precepts as part of the monastic discipline. Many monks ordain for a lifetime. Of these, a large percentage become scholars and teachers, while some specialise in healing and/or folk magic (although the latter is greatly discouraged by the current ruling party). There is no similar hermetic order for nuns, but women are welcome to reside in temples as lay nuns, with shaved heads and white robes.

The women only have to follow eight precepts. Because discipline for these 'nuns' is much less strenuous than it is for monks, they don't attain quite as high a social status as do monks. However, aside from the fact that they don't perform ceremonies on behalf of other lay persons, they engage in the same basic religious activities (meditation and study of dharma, ideal truth as set forth in the teaching of Buddha) as monks. The reality is that wats which draw sizeable contingents of eight-precept nuns are highly respected because women don't choose temples for reasons of clerical status – when more than a few reside at one temple it's because the teachings there are considered particularly strong.

Archaeologists have determined that before the 9th century, a period during which Sanskrit was used in ritual inscriptions, the Hinayana school constituted the prevalent form of Buddhism in Cambodia. Inscriptions and images indicate that Mahayana Buddhism was in favour after the 9th century but was replaced in the 13th century by a form of Hinayana Buddhism which arrived, along with the Pali language, from Sri Lanka via Thailand.

Between 1975 and 1979, the vast majority of Cambodia's Buddhist monks were murdered by the Khmer Rouge, who also damaged or destroyed virtually all of the country's more than 3000 wats. In the late 1980s, Buddhism was again made the state religion. At that time, Cambodia had about 6000 monks, who by law had to be at least 60 years old. The age requirements have been relaxed and young monks are once again a normal sight.

Islam

Cambodia's Muslims are descendants of Chams who migrated from what is now central Vietnam after the final defeat of the kingdom of Champa by the Vietnamese in 1471. Whereas their compatriots who remained in Vietnam were only partly Islamicised, the Cambodian Chams adopted a fairly orthodox version of Sunni Islam and maintained links with other Muslim communities in the region. Like their Buddhist neighbours, however, the Cham Muslims call the faithful to prayer by banging on a drum, rather than with the call of the muezzin, as in most Muslim lands.

Today, the Muslim community of Phnom Penh includes the descendants of people who

emigrated from Pakistan and Afghanistan several generations ago, and there is a neighbourhood of the city near Tuol Tom Pong Market still known as the 'Arab Village'. However, there are only about half-a-dozen Muslims fluent in Arabic, the language of the Koran, in all of Cambodia. In 1989, 20 Cambodian Muslims made the *hajj* (pilgrimage) to Mecca. *Halal* (killed according to Islamic law) meat is available in Phnom Penh in the O Russei, Tuol Tom Pong and Psar Cha markets.

A small heretical community known as the *Zahidin* follows traditions similar to those of the Muslim Chams of Vietnam, praying once a week (on Fridays) and observing Ramadan (a month of dawn-to-dusk fasting) only on the first, middle and last days of the month.

The Khmer Rouge seem to have made a concerted effort to annihilate Cambodia's Cham Muslim community.

Vietnamese Religions

During the 1920s, quite a few ordinary Cambodians became interested in Caodaism, a colourful syncretistic religion founded in Vietnam.

HOLIDAYS & FESTIVALS
Traditional Festivals

The dates of traditional Cambodian festivals are set according to the Khmer lunar calendar.

April
> *Chaul Chhnam* (mid-month) Three-day celebration of the Cambodian New Year.
> *Visak Bauchea* (late April) Commemorates the anniversary of the birth and illumination of the Buddha.

May
> *Chrat Prea Angkal* Ceremonial beginning of the sowing season.

September
> *Prachum Ben* (late September) People make offerings to the spirits of their ancestors.

October/November
> *Festival of the Reversing Current* (late October or early November) Also known as the Water Festival (Fête des Eaux), the Festival of the Reversing Current (in Khmer, Bon Om Touk or Sampeas Prea Khe) corresponds with the moment when the Tonlé Sap River, which since

July has been filling the Tonlé Sap Lake with the waters of the flood-swollen Mekong, reverses its flow and begins to empty the Tonlé Sap back into the Mekong. Pirogue (long canoe) races are held in Phnom Penh.

January/February

Tet (late January or early February) Tet, the Vietnamese and Chinese New Year, is celebrated by the country's ethnic-Vietnamese and ethnic-Chinese minorities. This week-long festival is a time for family reunions, the payment of debts, the avoidance of arguments, special foods, new clothes, flowers and new beginnings. Great importance is attached to starting the year properly because it is believed that the first day and first week of the new year will determine one's fortunes for the rest of the year.

Secular Holidays

Cambodia also has various secular holidays.

January

National Day (7th) Commemorates the Vietnamese overthrow of Pol Pot in 1979.

February

Anniversary of the signing of a treaty of friendship between Cambodia & Vietnam (18th) The treaty was signed in 1979.

April

Victory Day (17th) Commemorates the fall of the Lon Nol government in 1975.

May

International Workers' Day (1st) May Day.

Genocide Day (9th) Memorial day for the atrocities of the Khmer Rouge; ceremonies held at Choeung Ek and elsewhere.

June

Anniversary of the founding of the Revolutionary Armed Forces of Kampuchea (19th) Founded in 1951.

Anniversary of the founding of the People's Revolutionary Party of Cambodia (28th) Founded in 1951.

December

Anniversary of the Founding of the Front for National Reconstruction (FUNSK) (2nd) Founded in 1978.

Weddings The most popular months for weddings are June and July. Phnom Penhois who can afford it cover the pavement in front of their apartment buildings with a canvas awning, set up dozens of tables and hire a caterer to prepare copious quantities of food in huge kerbside cauldrons set over wood fires. Most such ceremonies are held on Sundays, the national day off, because more guests mean more gifts, which usually consist of cash.

LANGUAGE

For most Westerners, the writing and pronunciation of Cambodia's official language, Khmer, is both confusing and difficult. The Khmer writing system is about as different from Thai or Lao as Russian is from English.

There are 33 consonants and seemingly innumerable vowels. The consonants are divided into two series; the pronunciation of a vowel depends on which type of consonant precedes it. Eight different letters represent sounds that fall somewhere between the English letters 't' and 'd'. Two distinct sounds approximating the letter 'k' are represented by four letters; four other letters sound something like 'ch'.

Consonants written at the end of words are not fully released. That is, they are barely pronounced – almost dropped, but not quite. The final 'r' sometimes written at the end of words transliterated from Khmer is silent. Thus, *Angkor* is pronounced 'Angkoh' and *psar* becomes 'psah'.

For over a century, the second language of choice among educated Cambodians was French, and it is still spoken by many people who grew up before the 1970s. Recently, however, English has surged in popularity and is far more in demand among the students of the private language schools along 'English St' in Phnom Penh than is French.

Some people working in veterinary medicine received their training in Cuba and thus learned Spanish. A number of forestry experts learned German while studying in East Germany.

Some Useful Words & Phrases

Yes (used by men)

bat

 បាទ

Yes (used by women)

jas

ចា៎ះ

No
te
ទេ
Please
suom
សូម
Thank you
ar kun
អរគុណ

Greetings & Civilities

Hello
joom reab suor/suor sdei
ជំរាបសួរ/សួស្ដី
How are you?
tau neak sok sapbaiy jea te?
តើអ្នកសុខសប្បាយជាទេ?
Very well
sok touk jea thom-ada te
សុខទុក្ខជាធម្មតាទេ
Good night
rear trei suor sdei
រាត្រីសួស្ដី
Goodbye
lear heouy
លាហើយ
Excuse me
suom tous
សុំទោស

Accommodation

I want a ...
khjoom joung ban ...
ខ្ញុំចង់បាន ...
... single room
bantuop kre samrap mouy neak
...បន្ទប់គ្រែសម្រាប់ម្នាក់
... double room
bantuop kre samrap pee neak
...បន្ទប់គ្រែសម្រាប់ពីរនាក់
... triple room
bantuop samrap khnea pei neak
...បន្ទប់សម្រាប់គ្នាបីនាក់
... room with a bath
bantuop deil meen thlang gnout teouk
...បន្ទប់ដែលមានថ្លាងងូតទឹក
... room with a shower
bantuop deil meen teouk phka chouk
...បន្ទប់ដែលមានទឹកផ្កាឈូក

... bed
... kre mouy
...គ្រែមួយ
How much is a room?
chnoul mouy bantuop tleiy ponmaan?
ឈ្នួលមួយបន្ទប់ថ្លៃប៉ុន្មាន?
Could I see the room?
tau khjoom suom meul bantuop sen ban te?
តើខ្ញុំសុំមើលបន្ទប់សិនបានទេ?
Do you have anything cheaper?
tau neak meen eiy deil thuok jeang nees deir te?
តើអ្នកមានអ្វីដែលថោកជាងនេះដែរទេ?

Getting Around

Where is a/the ...?
tau ... nouv eir na?
តើ ... នៅឯណា?
... railway station
... sathani rout phleoung
... ស្ថានីយរថភ្លើង ...
... bus station
... ben lan
... បេនឡាន ...
... airport
... veal youn huos
... វាលយន្តហោះ ...
... ticket office
... kanleng luok suombuot
... កន្លែងលក់សំបុត្រ ...
... tourist office
... kariyaleiy samrap puok tesajor
... ការិយាល័យសម្រាប់ពួកទេសចរ ...
I want a ticket to ...
khjoom junh ban suombuot teou ...
ខ្ញុំចង់បានសំបុត្រទៅ ...
When does it depart?
tau ke jeng domneur moung ponmann?
តើគេចេញដំណើរម៉ោងប៉ុន្មាន?
When does it arrive here/there?
tau ke teou/mouk doul moung ponmaan?
តើគេទៅ/មកដល់ម៉ោងប៉ុន្មាន?
Is there an earlier/later one?
tau ke meen muon/krouy muoy nees deir reou te?
តើគេមានមុន/ក្រោយមួយនេះដែរឬទេ?
How many hours is the journey?
tau domneur nees sie pel ponmaan muong?
តើដំណើរនេះស៊ីពេលប៉ុន្មានម៉ោង?

bus
lan thom deouk monuos
ឡានធំដឹកមនុស្ស
train
rout phleoung
រថភ្លើង
boat
kopsl/tuok
កុប៉ាល់/ទូក

In the Country

town on the water
kompong
កំពង់
hill/mountain
phnom
ភ្នំ
lake
boeng
បឹង
river
tonley
ទន្លេ
pagoda/monastery
wat
វត្ត
sanctuary of a pagoda
vihear
វិហារ
marketplace
psar
ផ្សារ

Food

Is there any ...?
tau ke meen ... deir reou te?
តើគេមាន ... ដែរឬទេ?
... meat
... saach
... សាច់...
... fish
... trei
... ត្រី ...
... chicken
... maan
... មាន់ ...
... soup
... somlor/suop
... សំឡ/ស៊ុប ...

... noodles
... mee/kuy teav/moum banjuok
... មី/គុយទាវ/នំបញ្ចុក ...
I cannot eat ...
khjoom toam ...
ខ្ញុំតម ...
... monosodium glutamate
... masao suop
... ម្សៅស៊ុប
... any meat
... saach kruop yang
... សាច់គ្រប់យ៉ាង
... eggs
... poung sat
... ពងសត្វ
I eat chicken/fish
khjoom hope/tor toul tean saach maan/trei
ខ្ញុំហូប/ទទួលទាន សាច់មាន់/ត្រី

Emergencies

Please call ...
suom jouy hao ...
សូមជួយហៅ ...
... an ambulance
... lan peit
... ឡានពេទ្យ
... a doctor
... krou peit
... គ្រូពេទ្យ
... the police
... police
... ប៉ូលិស
... a dentist
... peit thamenh
... ពេទ្យធ្មេញ
I have ...
khjoom ...
ខ្ញុំ ...
... fever
... krun
... គ្រុន
... diarrhoea
... reak
... រាគ
... a cold
... padasay
... ផ្ដាសាយ

... a headache
  ... chheu kbal
  ... ឈឺក្បាល
... constipation
  ... toul leamouk
  ... ទល់លាមក
... diabetes
  ... meen rouk teouk nuom pa-em
  ... មានរោគទឹកនោមផ្អែម
... cramps
  ... romuol krapeu
  ... រមួលក្រពើ
It's an emergency.
  nees jea pheap ason
  នេះជាភាពអាសន្ន
I'm allergic to penicillin
  khjoom min trouv theat neoung thanam peneecilleen
  ខ្ញុំមិនត្រូវធាតុនឹងថ្នាំប៉េនីស៊ីលីន

Time & Dates
What time is it?
  eilov nees moung ponmaan?
  អីឡូវនេះម៉ោងប៉ុន្មាន?
When?
  pel na?
  ពេលណា?
What time?
  muong ponmaan?
  ម៉ោងប៉ុន្មាន?
morning
  preouk
  ព្រឹក
afternoon
  reuseal
  រសៀល
evening
  la-ngeech
  ល្ងាច
night
  yuop
  យប់
at night
  neouv pel yuop
  នៅពេលយប់
in the afternoon
  neouv pel reuseal
  នៅពេលរសៀល

in the evening
  neouv pel la-ngeech
  នៅពេលល្ងាច
in the morning
  neouv pel preouk
  នៅពេលព្រឹក
tomorrow
  sa-ek
  ស្អែក
yesterday
  masel menh
  ម្សិលមិញ
this week/month
  atit/khe nees
  អាទិត្យ/ខែនេះ
last week/month
  atit/khe muon
  អាទិត្យ/ខែ មុន
now
  eilov nees
  អីឡូវនេះ
What day is today?
  tha-ngai nees jea tha-ngai ei?
  ថ្ងៃនេះជាថ្ងៃអី?
What's today's date?
  tha-ngai nees trouv jea tha-ngai khe ei?
  ថ្ងៃនេះត្រូវជាថ្ងៃខែ អី?
Sunday
  tha-ngai atit
  ថ្ងៃអាទិត្យ
Monday
  tha-ngai chan
  ថ្ងៃចន្ទ
Tuesday
  tha-ngai angkea
  ថ្ងៃអង្គារ
Wednesday
  tha-ngai puot
  ថ្ងៃពុធ
Thursday
  tha-ngai preuo-haou
  ថ្ងៃព្រហស្បតិ៍
Friday
  tha-ngai sok
  ថ្ងៃសុក្រ
Saturday
  tha-ngai sav
  ថ្ងៃសៅរ៍

January
makara
មករា

February
kumphak
កុម្ភៈ

March
meenear
មិនា

April
mesa
មេសា

May
ou-saphea
ឧសភា

June
me-thuna
មិថុនា

July
kakkada
កក្កដា

August
seiha
សីហា

September
kanh-nha
កញ្ញា

October
tola
តុលា

November
vichika
វិច្ឆិកា

December
tha-nou
ធ្នូ

Numbers

1
mouy
១

2
pee
២

3
bei
៣

4
boun
៤

5
bram
៥

6
bram-mouy
៦

7
bram-pee
៧

8
bram-bei
៨

9
bran-boun
៩

10
duop
១០

11
duop-mouy
១១

12
duop-pee
១២

13
duop-bei
១៣

14
duop-boun
១៤

15
duop-bram
១៥

16
duop-bram-mouy
១៦

17
doup-bram-pee
១៧

18
doup-bram-bei
១៨

19
doup-bram-boun
១៩

20
maphei
២០

21
maphei-mouy
២១

30
samseb
៣០

40
sairseb
៤០

50
haseb
៥០

60
hokseb
៦០

70
jetseb
៧០

80
peitseb
៨០

90
kavseb
៩០

100
mouy-rouy
១០០

500
bram-rouy
៥០០

1000
mouy-paun
១០០០

10,000
mouy-meoun
១០,០០០

100,000
mouy-sen
១០០,០០០

100,000,000
mouy-rouy-lean
១០០,០០០,០០០

Foreign Countries

America
Amerik
អាមេរិក

American
Amerikang
អាមេរិកាំង

Australia
Prateh Ostralee
ប្រទេសអូស្ត្រាលី

Australian
Ostralee
អូស្ត្រាលី

England
Prateh Anglae
ប្រទេសអង់គ្លេស

English
Anglae
អង់គ្លេស

France
Prateh Barang
ប្រទេសបារាំង

French
Barang
បារាំង

Laos
Leeav
លាវ

Thailand
Prateh Thai
ប្រទេសថៃ

Thai
Thai
ថៃ

Vietnam
Vietnam
វៀតណាម

Prateh, which is related to the Lao *pathet* (as in Pathet Lao) and the Hindi *pradesh* (as in Uttar Pradesh or Himachal Pradesh), means 'land' or 'land of'. Thus, France is rendered *Prateh Barang*, 'Land of the French'. The word *srok* is sometimes used in place of *prateh*.

An English word of recent Cambodian mintage is 'Polpotites', which is used to refer to the protégés of Pol Pot, the murderous leader of the Khmer Rouge, who are held responsible by the Phnom Penh government for the atrocities committed between 1975 and 1979. These atrocities are not solely attributed to the Khmer Rouge because many of the leaders of the present government in Phnom Penh served as Khmer Rouge officers before turning against Pol Pot.

Transport (TW)

Market scenes (TW)

Facts for the Visitor

VISAS & EMBASSIES

Although Cambodian diplomatic representation overseas is still very limited, visas are rapidly becoming easier to obtain. For most independent travellers Bangkok in Thailand and Ho Chi Minh City (Saigon) in Vietnam are the popular places for obtaining a visa.

Travellers arriving from Bangkok currently prearrange their visa in Bangkok when booking their flight. This process takes about a week and the visas are then issued on arrival at Pochentong Airport, Phnom Penh. You must have three passport photos with you when you arrive. Similarly, from Singapore you can obtain a visa through Airtrust, who operate the weekly flight to Phnom Penh, but the procedure takes about two weeks and costs US$100.

The other popular alternative is to make a side trip into Cambodia from Ho Chi Minh City. Visas can be obtained from the Cambodian Consulate in Ho Chi Minh City at a cost of US$8. The visa takes seven days to issue and usually requires several visits to the consulate. This means that you must be prepared to hang around in the south of Vietnam for a week waiting for the visa to be issued.

Some travellers have applied for their visa at the Cambodian Embassy in Hanoi and arranged to collect it from the Cambodian Consulate in Ho Chi Minh City after travelling there.

It's probably hopeless, but it is theoretically possible to request a visa by writing to the Ministry of Foreign Affairs, Phnom Penh, State of Cambodia.

Visa Extensions

Visa extensions are granted by the Foreign Ministry (☎ 2.4641, 2.3241, 2.4441) in Phnom Penh, which is on the western side of Quai Karl Marx at 240 St. The process may take three or more days.

Cambodian Embassies

The Cambodian government still has only limited diplomatic representation abroad although that should start to change, particularly as progress is made towards the scheduled UN-supervised elections in 1993. Meanwhile, the most useful Cambodian consular sections are those in Laos and Vietnam.

Bulgaria
    Blvd Salvador Allende 2, Sofia (☎ 75-71-35)
Cuba
    Avenida 5a, Miramar, Havana (☎ 296779)
Czechoslovakia
    Na Hubalcé 1, 16900 Prague 6 (☎ (2) 352603)
Hungary
    Rath Gyögy v 48, Budapest XII (☎ 151-878)
India
    C4/4 Paschimi Marg, Vasant Vihar, New Delhi 110057 (☎ (11) 608595)
Laos
    Thanon Saphan Thong Neua, Vientiane (☎ 2750, 4527)
Mongolia
    Ulan Bator
Russia
    Strarokonyushenny per 16, Moscow (☎ (095) 201-21-15)
Vietnam
    71 Tran Hung Dao St, Hanoi (☎ 53788/9). The embassy is open Monday to Saturday from 8 to 11 am and from 2 to 4.30 pm. It is possible to apply for a visa here and pick it up at the consulate in Saigon.
    41 Phung Khac Khoan St, Saigon (☎ 92751/2, 92744). The consulate is open Monday to Saturday from 8 to 11 am and from 2 to 5 pm.

MONEY

US$1   =   800r
A$1   =   600r
UK£1   =   1400r
Thai B1 =   40r

Currency

Cambodia's currency is the riel, abbreviated here by a lower-case 'r' written after the sum. From around 200r to the US dollar in mid-1989 the black market rate rocketed to 800r to the dollar within three years but now appears to be slowing.

The US dollar operates virtually as a

second currency in Cambodia and many tourist services are priced in US dollars. A restaurant popular with foreigners may, for example, allow you to pay in riels or dollars and will give you change in either currency. Taking riels into or out of the country is forbidden. Gold is used for many larger transactions.

The Khmer Rouge abolished currency and blew up the National Bank building in Phnom Penh. For 15 months after the overthrow of the Pol Pot regime in January 1979, goods and services were bartered or exchanged for gold or hard currencies. New riel notes were issued in March 1980. Many of the large old Cambodian notes ended their useful life glued together to make paper bags.

Salaries

Government workers receive monthly salaries equivalent to less than US$5. As a result, civil servants at all levels must either take bribes or moonlight in order to survive.

Every month government employees can purchase – at highly subsidised prices – 18 kg of rice (and 10 kg per child), two blocks of Russian-made soap, one kg of sugar, one tin of sweetened condensed milk (if available) and, at times, other goods as well. Every year, the state sells each worker one complete set of clothes. The unemployed or self-employed must purchase these staples on the open market.

Changing Money

By far the most useful foreign currency in Cambodia is the US dollar, though the Foreign Trade Bank of Cambodia (in French, Banque du Commerce Extérieur du Cambodge; formerly the National People's Bank), also changes pounds sterling, French francs, Australian dollars, Canadian dollars, Deutschmarks and Swiss francs.

At present, they do *not* handle Hong Kong dollars, Japanese yen, Singapore dollars or Thai baht. They can, however, change US dollar-denominated international money orders and travellers' cheques issued by American Express, Barclays, Citicorp, Thomas Cook and VISA; there is a 2% commission.

Official currency exchange services are not available at the Moc Bai border crossing between Vietnam and Cambodia, though passers-by and vendors at the Neak Luong

Ferry will exchange dong (the currency of Vietnam) for riels at a rate only about 10% less than that of Phnom Penh.

Black Market The variation between official and black market rates is narrowing, although you can find vastly worse rates at tourist hotels. Unofficial moneychangers operate very openly from shops or in the markets – large stacks of riels in glass cases are a positive sign that you've found the appropriate place. Riels can also be changed back into US dollars on the black market for marginally less than the going dollars-to-riels rate.

Cheques The Foreign Trade Bank can theoretically cash travellers' cheques and even personal cheques but, because they have to be sent to Paris, it will take many weeks to credit your account.

Money Transfers

It is possible to wire money from abroad to the Foreign Trade Bank, but it can be picked up in Phnom Penh only in riels or used to pay hotel bills and the like. Such transfers, which are routed through the Banque Nationale de Paris, take a month or two to complete. Banks with transfer agreements with the National People's Bank of Cambodia include:

Australia
    Commonwealth Bank of Australia (Sydney)
Belgium
    Banque Bruxelles Lambert (Brussels)
Canada
    Banque Nationale de Paris (Montreal)
    Canadian Imperial Bank of Commerce, (Toronto)
France
    Banque Commerciale pour l'Europe du Nord, 79-81 Blvd Haussmann, 75382 (Paris)
    Banque d'Indochine et de Suez, 96 Blvd Haussmann, 75008 (Paris)
    Banque Nationale de Paris, 16 Blvd des Italiens (Paris)
    Banque Worms, 45 Blvd Haussmann, 75427 (Paris)
    Crédit Commercial de France, 103 Ave des Champs Élysées, 75008 (Paris)

Germany
    Dresdner Bank A G (Frankfurt)
    Deutsche Bank A G (Frankfurt)
Hong Kong
    Banque Nationale de Paris, PO Box 763 (Hong Kong)
Laos
    Banque pour le Commerce Extérieur Lao, 1 Pangkham Rd or PO Box 84 (Vientiane)
Russia
    State Bank of the USSR, Neglinaya 12, (Moscow)
    Bank for Foreign Economic Affairs of the USSR, Kopievski Lane 3/5 (Moscow)
Singapore
    Moscow Narodny Bank Ltd, MNB Building, 50 Robinson Rd, 0106
    Banque Worms (Singapore Branch), 50 Raffles Place, 16-01 Shell Tower, 0104
Switzerland
    Union Bank of Switzerland (Zürich)
UK
    Moscow Narodny Bank Ltd, 24-32 King William St (London)
    Midland Bank Ltd (London)
USA
    Banque Nationale de Paris (New York Branch), 499 Park Ave, New York, NY 10022
Vietnam
    State Bank of Vietnam, 47-49 Ly Thai To St (Hanoi)
    Bank for Foreign Trade of Vietnam, 47-49 Ly Thai To St (Hanoi) and 17 Ben Chuong Duong St (Ho Chi Minh City)

Costs

Meals cost only US$1 to US$3 everywhere except in the fanciest restaurants. Hotel accommodation in Phnom Penh and Siem Reap typically costs from US$10 to US$30 a night although it's now quite possible to spend over US$100 a night in Phnom Penh. Public transport (buses, trains) is cheap but off-limits to foreigners. Hiring a car will set you back at least US$20 a day.

All this will be included if you book a tour, for which you'll pay up to US$200 a day.

Tipping

Tipping is not expected but is very much appreciated, especially by people whose total monthly government salary may total less than US$5.

WHAT TO BRING

Aside from what is necessary on any trip, travellers to Cambodia may want to consider bringing the following:

a pocket short-wave radio – Bangkok newspapers are becoming more readily available in Phnom Penh, and the Hotel Cambodiana even has CNN (Cable News Network), but otherwise short-wave broadcasts of the BBC, VOA, Radio Australia, etc, are the only source of hard news

reading material (very little in English is available)

a French-English English-French dictionary (useful for communicating with older Cambodians who were educated under the French)

a torch (flashlight) for use during frequent power outages and when visiting caves

batteries

water purification tablets

a canteen (in which you can treat water with water purification tablets)

a money belt (the best kind is worn inside your pants or skirt)

a small cable lock (for locking up a rented bicycle)

official letters of introduction

extra visa photos, although these are readily and cheaply obtained in Cambodia

small-denomination US dollar bills, as the dollar is virtually a second currency in Cambodia

small gifts

Thai postage stamps so foreigners heading to Bangkok can mail your postcards and letters for you

enough film for the whole trip (only colour print film is regularly available)

laundry soap (even if you have someone else do your laundry, they may not use detergent unless you provide it)

thongs for the shower

tampons & sanitary napkins

contraceptives

a first-aid kit

malaria prophylactics (see your physician for details and a prescription)

Pepto Bismol or some similar medications, including perhaps a general antibiotic

a mosquito net (necessary only if you will be staying somewhere other than in hotels – even the cheapest dives have them)

a collapsible umbrella and other rain gear (for the monsoon season only)

TOURISM INFORMATION
Local Tourist Offices

For information on the General Directorate of Tourism and Phnom Penh Tourism, see the Information section in the Phnom Penh chapter. Information on Angkor Tourism and Angkor Conservation are listed under Siem Reap in the Angkor chapter.

Non-Governmental Organisations

Non-governmental humanitarian aid organisations working in Cambodia (each followed by its acronym and the city in which its headquarters is located) include:

American Friends Service Committee (AFSC; Philadelphia)

Australian Catholic Relief (ACR; Sydney)

Australian Red Cross Society (ARCS; Melbourne)

Church World Services (CWS; New York)

Coopération Internationale pour le Développement et la Solidarité (CIDSE; Brussels)

Enfance Espoir (Choicy Le Roi, France)

Enfants du Cambodge (EdC; Paris)

French Red Cross (Croix-Rouge Française, or CRF; Paris)

Groupe de Recherche et d'Échanges Technologiques (GRET; Paris)

International Committee of the Red Cross (ICRC, in French, Comité International de la Croix-Rouge, or CICR; Geneva)

International Rice Research Institute (IRRI; Manila)

Japan International Volunteer Centre (JVC; Tokyo)

Joint Australian NGO Office (JANGOO; Darlinghurst, NSW)

Lutheran World Service (LWS; Geneva)

Medical & Scientific Aid for Vietnam, Laos & Kampuchea (MSAVLK; London)

Mennonite Central Committee (MCC; Akron, Pennsylvania)

Operation Handicap International (OHI; Brussels)

Oxfam (Oxford, England)

Partnership for Development in Kampuchea (PADEK; The Hague)

Quaker Service Australia (QSA; Hobart)

Redd Barna (Norwegian Save the Children; Oslo)

Swedish Red Cross (Svenska Röda Korset, or SRC; Stockholm)

Swiss Red Cross (Schweizerisches Rotes Kreuz, or Croix-Rouge Suisse; Berne)

United Nations Children's Fund (UNICEF; New York)

United Nations High Commission for Refugees (UNHCR; Geneva)

World Council of Churches (WCC; Geneva)

World Food Programme (WFP, in French, Programme Alimentaire Mondial, or PAM; Rome)

World Vision International (WVI; Monrovia, California)

GENERAL INFORMATION
Post

Although Cambodia's postal rates are far more reasonable than those in Vietnam (an airmail postcard overseas costs less than US$0.25), service is extremely slow because all international mail (except that to parts of eastern Asia and Australia, which goes through Saigon) is routed via Moscow, and there are only three or four flights to Moscow each month.

Letters sent to Cambodia from abroad take two to three months to arrive.

Telephone

Surprisingly, Phnom Penh is not such a bad place to make international calls. The tariffs are high but still much lower than in Vietnam, and because of the direct Interspoutnik satellite link with Moscow, the wait is sometimes only a matter of minutes.

The minimum length of a telephone call is three minutes, which from Phnom Penh will cost from US$11.40 to Australia and US$16.95 to the USA. Telephone calls into Cambodia are routed through either Hanoi or Moscow; calls out of the country go through Moscow, using Phnom Penh's Interspoutnik satellite link-up (the ground station is one block north of the railway station).

Theoretically, there is a domestic telephone service from Phnom Penh to all of Cambodia's provinces except Koh Kong, Kratie, Mondulkiri, Preah Vihear, Ratanakiri and Stung Treng. In practice, making calls around the country is virtually impossible. In 1981, the country only had 7000 telephones.

Telex, Telegraph & Fax

Telegrams (sent by teletype) to Australia, North America and Western Europe cost US$0.60 to US$1 per word. There were plans to establish international telex links by 1990. Most domestic inter-provincial communication is presently carried out by telegram.

Interest in improving Cambodia's telecommunications facilities has been shown by the Australians (who have done similar work in Vietnam and Laos), the French, the Japanese, the Thais and even the Americans (through the Thai subsidiaries of American companies).

Time

Cambodia, like Vietnam, Thailand and Laos, is seven hours ahead of GMT. When it is noon in Cambodia it is 5 am in London, 3 pm in Sydney, 1 am in New York and 10 pm the previous evening in San Francisco.

Electricity

Electricity in Phnom Penh and most of the rest of Cambodia is 220 volts, 50 Hz (cycles). Even in Phnom Penh, there may be several power outages a day, so it makes sense to have a torch (flashlight) and candles handy after dark. Outside of the capital, there may be electric power only in the evenings, usually from about 6.30 to 9.30 pm. This situation is changing and Siem Reap now has 24-hour power, apart from the odd breakdown.

Because most night-time lighting in Cambodia's homes is provided by tiny kerosene lamps rather than electric bulbs (even in the capital few buildings have electricity), the country produces very little light pollution of the sort that ruins star-gazing in many other places around the world. A glance skyward at night will reveal a twinkling intergalactic panorama of stars, galaxies (including a very milky-looking Milky Way) and shooting stars.

Business Hours

Government offices, which are open Monday to Saturday, theoretically begin the working day at 7 or 7.30 am, breaking for a siesta from 11 or 11.30 am to 2 or 2.30 pm and ending the day at 5.30 pm. However, it is a safe bet that few people will be around early in the morning or after 4 or 4.30 pm.

In keeping with Cambodia's revolutionary ideology, all workers – including government bureaucrats of all ranks – must spend at least one day a week doing manual labour. One often sees Phnom Penh's white collar workers toiling in the fields, staring off into the distance and occasionally taking a whack at the earth.

Laundry

You can usually find a hotel attendant to do your laundry. They may try to clean your clothes by hand without the benefit of soap unless you provide some. Settle on the price beforehand.

Weights & Measures

Cambodia uses the metric system. For those unaccustomed to this system, there is a metric/imperial conversion chart at the end of the book.

BOOKS

Angkor

A number of superb works on Angkor have been published over the years. *Angkor: An Introduction* (Oxford University Press, Hong Kong, 1963; reissued by Oxford University Press, Singapore, 1986) by George Coedes gives excellent background information on Angkorian Khmer civilisation. You might also look for Malcolm MacDonald's *Angkor & the Khmers* (Jonathan Cape, 1958; reissued by Oxford University Press, Singapore, 1987); *Arts & Civilization of Angkor*

(Fredrick A Prager, New York, 1958) by Bernard Groslier & Jacques Arthaud; and, in French, *Histoire d'Angkor* (Presses Universitaires de France, Paris, 1974) by Madeleine Giteau.

The 3rd edition of *Angkor, Guide Henri Parmentier* (EKLIP/Albert Portail, Phnom Penh, 1959/1960) by Henri Parmentier, probably the best guidebook to Angkor ever written, was published in both English and French. A recent English-language reprint, entitled *Henri Parmentier's Guide to Angkor* has been produced in Phnom Penh by the publisher EKLIP. It's readily available in Phnom Penh or Siem Reap, although the price varies considerably from as little as US$5 from street vendors to as much as US$10 or even US$15 in hotels.

The Art of Southeast Asia by Philip Rawson (Thames & Hudson, 1967) has recently been reprinted for Asia Books in Thailand and has excellent chapters on Angkor. *Angkor* by Michael Freeman & Roger Warner (Houghton Mifflin, 1990) is a big, glossy, coffee-table book on Angkor.

In English, you might also look for *Angkor* (Librairie Renouard et H Laurens, Paris, 1933) by George Groslier, and the even more antiquated *Guide to the Ruins of Angkor* (Imprimerie d'Extrême Orient, Hanoi, 1913). Other useful publications include *Tourist Guide to Saigon, Phnom Penh & Angkor* (Imprimerie Nouvelle Albert Portail, Saigon, 1930) and *Petit Guide d'Angkor* (Bureau du Tourisme en Indochine, 1929). *Les Monuments du Groupe d'Angkor* by Maurice Glaize (Albert Portail, Saigon, 1948) is a French work with detailed histories, descriptions and maps.

I highly recommend that travellers serious about learning something of Khmer civilisation while visiting Angkor track down one of these works.

History

The most comprehensive work in English on Cambodian history is *The Ancient Khmer Empire* by L P Briggs (1951). Also useful for historical background is *The Indianized States of South-East Asia* by George Coedes

(1968), originally published in French as *Les États Hindouisés d'Indochine et d'Indonésie* (2nd edition, 1964). Also worthwhile is *A History of Cambodia* by David P Chandler (Westview Press, Boulder, Colorado, 1983).

The expansion of the Vietnam War onto Cambodian territory and events through the mid-1970s are superbly documented by William Shawcross in his award-winning book *Sideshow: Kissinger, Nixon & the Destruction of Cambodia* (The Hogarth Press, London, and Simon & Schuster, New York, 1979).

Cambodia: Year Zero (1978) by François Ponchaud (originally published in French as *Cambodge: Année Zéro* in 1977) is an account of life in Cambodia under the Khmer Rouge. Other works on this period include *The Stones Cry Out: A Cambodian Childhood, 1975-1980* (Hill & Wang, New York, 1986) by Molyda Szymusiak, originally published in French as *Les Pierres Crieront: Une Enfance Cambodgienne, 1975-1980* (La Découverte, Paris, 1984); *The Cambodian Agony* (1987) by David Ablin; and *The Murderous Revolution* (1985) by Martin Stuart-Fox.

The atrocities of the Khmer Rouge are documented by *Kampuchea, Decade of Genocide: Report of the Finnish Enquiry Commission* (Zed Books, London, 1984) edited by Kimmo Kiljunen. *Brother Enemy* (Collier, 1986), an excellent work by Nayan Chanda, examines events in Indochina since 1975.

William Shawcross' work *The Quality of Mercy: Cambodia, Holocaust & Modern Conscience* (André Deutsch, UK, and Simon & Schuster, USA, 1984) looks at the contradictions inherent in the massive international famine-relief operation mounted in 1979 and 1980. This still highly relevant title is available in Thailand in a paperback edition published by DD Books.

National Geographic

National Geographic articles on Cambodia include the following (listed chronologically): 'Forgotten Ruins of Indochina'

(March 1912, pp 209-72); 'Enigma of Cambodia' and 'Four Glimpses of Siva: The Mystery of Angkor' (September 1928, pp 303-32); 'Under the French Tricololor in Indochina' (Aug 1931, pp 166-99); 'By Motor Trail Across French Indochina' and 'Tricolor Rules the Rainbow in French Indochina' (Oct 1935, pp 487-534); 'Strife-Torn Indochina' (Oct 1950, pp 599-51); 'Portrait of Indochina' (April 1951, pp 461-90); 'Indochina Faces the Dragon' (Sept 1952, pp 287-328); 'Angkor, Jewel of the Jungle' (April 1960, pp 517-69); 'Cambodia, Indochina's 'Neutral' Corner' (Oct 1964, pp 514-51); 'The Mekong, River of Terror & Hope' (Dec 1968, pp 737-87); 'The Lands & Peoples of South-East Asia' (March 1971, pp 295-365); 'The Temples of Angkor' (May 1982, pp 548-89) and 'Kampuchea Wakens from a Nightmare' (May 1982, pp 590-623). Some of the articles on Angkor, most of which are accompanied by *National Geographic's* usual fine illustrations and maps, may be worth bringing along to read on the spot.

Readers of French may want to take a look at the March 1988 issue of the magazine *Dossiers Histoire et Archéologie*, which is dedicated to 'Angkor – L'Art Khmer au Cambodge et en Thaïlande'.

Politics & Society

Kampuchea: Politics, Economics & Society (Frances Pinter, London & Lynne Rienner, Boulder, Colorado, 1988) by Michael Vickery, and *Indochina: Vietnam, Laos, Cambodia*, a 'Country Profile' published annually in London and New York by the Economist Intelligence Unit, have some of the best up-to-date information available on Cambodia's changing social and political system. Eva Mysliwiec's *Punishing the Poor: The International Isolation of Kampuchea* (Oxfam, Oxford, England, 1988) looks at Cambodia's status of diplomatic pariahdom.

Ethnic Groups of Mainland South-East Asia edited by Frank M Lebar (1964) is a good source of information on Cambodia's ethno-linguistic minority peoples. *The Chinese in Cambodia* (1967) by W E Willmott takes a look at Cambodia's ethnic-Chinese minority.

Travel & Travel Guides

This volume is the most comprehensive travel guidebook to Cambodia on the market. Lonely Planet also publishes *Vietnam, Laos & Cambodia – a travel survival kit* which combines information on Cambodia with the other two countries of Indochina.

Excellent information on Cambodia's archaeological sites – in some cases, however, superseded by subsequent research – is provided by the classic guidebooks to Indochina published by Claudius Madrolle before WW II, copies of which may be available at major university libraries.

To Angkor (Société d'Éditions Géographiques, Maritimes et Coloniales, Paris, 1939) is the English version of the French work *Vers Angkor* (Librairie Hachette,

Paris, 1925). *Indochina* (Société d'Éditions Géographiques, Maritimes et Coloniales, Paris, 1939), an English-language condensation of the two-volume set *Indochine du Nord* and *Indochine du Sud*, has the same spread on Cambodia as *To Angkor*. The most comprehensive section on Cambodia is to be found in the excellent 2nd augmented edition of *Indochine du Sud* (Société d'Éditions Géographiques, Maritimes et Coloniales, Paris, 1939).

Francophone fans of antiquarian books may want to track down *Voyage au Cambodge* by L Delaporte (Librairie C Delgrave, Paris, 1880). Norman Lewis' *A Dragon Apparent* (originally published 1951, available in paperback from Eland Books) is a classic account of a 1950 foray into an Indochina which was soon to disappear. In the course of his travels, Norman Lewis makes a circuit from Phnom Penh around the Tonlé Sap with a pause in Angkor. A more recent travelogue is *The Road to Angkor*, an entertaining work by Christopher Pym (Robert Hale, London, 1959).

MAPS

Old maps of Cambodia may be available in Phnom Penh. On Vietnamese maps of the country, the Khmer characters are translated into the Latin-based Vietnamese alphabet. The Nelles Verlag *Vietnam, Laos & Kampuchea* map at 1:1,500,000 scale is the best readily available international map of the country.

MEDIA
Newspapers & Magazines

Restrictions on the domestic press have recently been relaxed. Foreign newspapers and magazines are becoming more readily available, and Bangkok newspapers can usually be obtained the same day in Phnom Penh.

Radio

The daily English broadcast on Voice of Vietnam from Hanoi is from 6 to 6.30 pm on 1010 kHz on the medium-wave (AM) band. In Phnom Penh, radio frequencies to try for domestic programming include 82.2 MHz, 92.1 MHz, 94.3 MHz, 98.3 MHz and 103.7 MHz on the FM band and 920 kHz and 1300 kHz on medium wave (AM band).

With a short-wave receiver, news, music and feature programmes in a multitude of languages can easily be picked up, especially at night. Reception of any given broadcast depends on a variety of variable factors, including ionospheric conditions and sunspot activity. Frequencies you might try for English-language broadcasts include:

Radio Australia
17,750 kHz, 15,415 kHz, 15,395 kHz, 15,240 kHz, 15,140 kHz, 11,705 kHz, 9770 kHz, 9645 kHz and 7205 kHz
BBC World Service
15,360 kHz (in the early morning); 15,280 kHz (during the day); and 15,310 kHz, 11,750 kHz, 9740 kHz and 6195 kHz (at night). Other frequencies include 11,955 kHz, 7145 kHz, 5975 kHz and 3915 kHz
Voice of America
17,730 kHz and 15,215 kHz (in the morning); 11,755 kHz (in the evening); 6110 kHz, 9760 kHz and 15,760 kHz (at night)
Christian Science Monitor Radio
17,780 kHz (around noon)

FILM & PHOTOGRAPHY

Do not put film of any speed or type through the ancient X-ray machines at the airports in Phnom Penh, Saigon or Hanoi.

The Cambodians are not particularly restrictive about what you can photograph, but use common sense about taking pictures of soldiers, fortifications, military vehicles, airports, etc. It is always best to ask people – especially monks – if they mind your photographing them before you whip out your camera and shove it in their face.

You can easily run through lots of film in Cambodia, so if you're a keen photographer come well supplied. Modern photo labs offering quick processing of colour print film have already sprung up in Phnom Penh.

HEALTH

Travel health depends on your predeparture preparations, your day-to-day health care while travelling and how you handle any medical problem or emergency that may develop.

Cambodia has one of the world's highest infant mortality rates – of every 1000 Cambodian newborns, as many as 200 die before their first birthday. Because of malnutrition, contaminated water supplies and a very limited public health infrastructure, Cambodians' life expectancy has fallen from 42 years for men and 44 years for women in 1970 to approximately 36 years for men and 39 years for women today.

Travel Health Guides

Travellers' Health by Dr Richard Dawood (Oxford University Press) is comprehensive, easy to read and authoritative but rather large to lug around. *Staying Healthy in Asia, Africa & Latin America* by Volunteers in Asia and *The Pocket Doctor* by Stephen Bezruchka (The Mountaineers) are handy pocket-size travel health guides.

Predeparture Preparations

Health Insurance A travel insurance policy to cover theft, loss and medical problems is a good idea. There is a wide variety of policies and your travel agent will make specific recommendations.

Medical Kit It is wise to carry a small, straightforward medical kit. A possible kit list includes:

• Aspirin or Panadol – for pain or fever
• Antihistamine (such as Benadryl) – useful as a decongestant for colds, allergies, to ease the itch from insect bites or stings, or to help prevent motion sickness
• Antibiotics – they must be prescribed and you should carry the prescription with you
• Kaolin preparation (Pepto-Bismol), Imodium or Lomotil – for stomach upsets
• Rehydration mixture – for treatment of severe diarrhoea, which is particularly important if travelling with children
• Antiseptic, mercurochrome and antibiotic powder or similar 'dry' spray – for cuts and grazes
• Calamine lotion – to ease irritation from bites or stings
• Bandages and Band-aids – for minor injuries
• Scissors, tweezers and a thermometer (note that mercury thermometers are prohibited by airlines)

• Insect repellent, sunscreen, suntan lotion, chap stick and water purification tablets

Ideally, antibiotics should be administered only under medical supervision and should never be taken indiscriminately.

Overuse of antibiotics can weaken your body's ability to deal with infections naturally and can reduce the drug's efficacy on a future occasion. Take only the recommended dose at the prescribed intervals and continue using the antibiotic for the prescribed period, even if the illness seems to be cured earlier. Antibiotics are specific to the infections they can treat. Stop immediately if you have any serious reactions to the antibiotics, and don't use them at all if you are unsure whether you have the correct one.

In countries like Cambodia if a medicine is available at all it will generally be available over the counter and the price will be much cheaper than in the West. However, be wary of buying drugs, particularly where the expiry date may have passed or correct storage conditions may not have been observed. It's possible that drugs which are no longer recommended (or have even been banned) in the West may still be dispensed. Pharmacies in Cambodia are marked with a blue cross outlined in white, often painted on a blue awning.

Health Preparations Make sure you're healthy before you start travelling. If you wear glasses or contact lenses, take a spare pair and your prescription. If you require a particular medication take an adequate supply. Take the prescription, with the generic rather than the brand name, as it will make getting replacements easier.

Immunisations Although there are no vaccination entry requirements for Cambodia, the country's health problems are sufficiently severe to make some immunisations worthwhile. Vaccinations should be recorded on an International Health Certificate; even if you don't have to show it to anybody, it's a useful record.

Plan ahead if getting vaccinations – some

of them require an initial shot followed by a booster, and some vaccinations should not be given together. Most travellers from Western countries will have been immunised against various diseases during childhood, but your doctor may still recommend booster shots against measles or polio. The period of protection offered by vaccinations differs widely and some are contraindicated if you are pregnant.

A possible list of vaccinations includes:

Cholera – Cholera vaccination is only likely to be required if you are coming from an infected area. Protection is not very effective, only lasts six months and is contraindicated for pregnancy

Infectious Hepatitis – Gamma globulin has proven very successful in reducing the chances of hepatitis infection. Because it may interfere with the development of immunity, it should not be given until at least 10 days after administration of the last vaccine needed.

Other Vaccinations – Smallpox has been wiped out worldwide, so immunisation is not necessary. Tetanus and diphtheria boosters are necessary every 10 years and protection is highly recommended. Typhoid vaccinations last for three years and are useful if you are travelling for long in rural areas.

Basic Rules

Taking care in what you eat and drink is the most important health rule; stomach upsets are the most likely travel health problem but the majority of these upsets will be relatively minor. Don't become paranoid – trying the local food is part of the experience.

Water The number one rule is *don't drink the water* and that includes ice. If you don't know for certain that the water is safe, always assume the worst – reputable brands of bottled water or soft drinks are generally fine, although in some places bottles may have been refilled with tap water. Take care with fruit juice, particularly if water may have been added. Milk should be treated with suspicion, but you rarely find milk in Cambodia anyway. If you want milk for tea or coffee, it will probably be condensed milk from a can. Tea or coffee should also be OK, since the water should have been boiled.

Clean your teeth with purified water rather than water straight from the tap.

Water Purification The simplest way to purify water is to boil it thoroughly, which means boiling for 10 minutes, something which happens very rarely. Simple filtering doesn't remove all dangerous organisms, so if you cannot boil water it should be treated chemically. Chlorine tablets (Puritabs, Steritabs or other brand names) will kill many but not all pathogens. Iodine is very effective in purifying water and is available in tablet form (such as Potable Aqua), but follow the directions carefully and remember that too much iodine can be harmful.

If you can't find tablets, two drops of tincture of iodine (2%) per litre or quart of clear water is the recommended dosage; the treated water should be left to stand for 30 minutes before drinking. Using iodine crystals is more complicated as you have first to prepare a saturated iodine solution. Iodine loses its effectiveness if exposed to air or damp, so keep it in an air-tight container.

Food Salads and fruit should be washed with purified water or peeled where possible. Ice cream is usually OK if it is a reputable brand name (unlikely in Cambodia), but be wary of street vendors and of ice cream that has melted and been refrozen. Thoroughly cooked food is safest but not if it has been left to cool or been reheated.

Take great care with shellfish or fish and avoid undercooked meat. In general, places that are packed with travellers or locals will be fine, whereas empty restaurants are questionable. The food served in Cambodia's better restaurants is usually healthy.

Health Care Many health problems can be avoided by taking care of yourself. Wash your hands frequently, as it's quite easy to contaminate your own food.

In the hot season, make sure you drink enough – don't rely on feeling thirsty to indicate when you should drink. Not needing to urinate or very dark-yellow urine is a danger sign. Always carry a water bottle with you on long trips. Excessive sweating can lead to loss of salt and, therefore, muscle cramping. Salt tablets are not a good idea as a preventative but in places where salt is not used much, adding salt to food can help.

You can also avoid potential diseases by dressing sensibly. Worm infections can occur if you walk barefoot. You can avoid insect bites by covering bare skin when insects are around, by screening windows or beds or by using insect repellents.

Last but not least, don't be too concerned with your health. Few people have any real problems.

Medical Problems & Treatment
Self-diagnosis and treatment can be risky, so wherever possible seek qualified help. Although we do give treatment dosages, they are for emergency use only. Medical advice should be sought before administering any drugs. An embassy, consulate or five-star hotel is usually able to recommend a good place to go for such advice.

Standards of medical attention in Cambodia are not high, so for serious ailments the best advice is to get on a plane and head for Bangkok. Cambodia's hospitals suffer from chronic shortages of almost everything. Not only must patients purchase their own medication on the black market (most hospitals stock virtually no pharmaceuticals), but some provincial hospitals are so impoverished that people who need surgery must purchase soap for the doctors to scrub-up with, fluid to sterilise the scalpels and petrol for the generator that powers the lights in the operating theatre.

If you need surgery, you're best off going to Bangkok, as the surgeons in Phnom Penh are probably OK, but anaesthesia may not be handled properly. Most intravenous solutions in Cambodian hospitals are *not* sterile and should definitely be avoided.

Climatic & Geographical Considerations
Sunburn In the tropics, you can get sunburnt surprisingly quickly, even through cloud, so use a sunscreen. A hat provides added protection, and you should also use zinc cream

or some other barrier cream for your nose and lips. Calamine lotion is good for mild sunburn.

Prickly Heat Prickly heat is an itchy rash caused by excessive perspiration trapped under the skin. It usually strikes people who have just arrived in a hot climate and whose pores have not yet opened sufficiently to cope with increased perspiration. Keeping cool but bathing often, using a mild talcum powder or even resorting to air-conditioning may help until you acclimatise.

Heat Exhaustion Salt deficiency or dehydration can cause heat exhaustion. Take time to acclimatise to high temperatures and make sure you get sufficient liquids. Vomiting or diarrhoea can deplete your liquid and salt levels.

Fungal Infections To prevent hot weather fungal infections, wear loose, comfortable clothes, avoid artificial fibres, wash frequently and dry carefully. If you do get an infection, wash the infected area daily with a disinfectant or medicated soap and water, and rinse and dry well. Apply an antifungal powder like the widely available Tinaderm. Try to expose the infected area to air or sunlight as much as possible and wash all towels and underwear in hot water as well as changing them often.

Diseases of Insanitation

Diarrhoea A change of water, food or climate can all cause the runs. Diarrhoea caused by contaminated food or water is more serious. A few rushed toilet trips with no other symptoms is not indicative of a serious problem. Dehydration is the main danger with diarrhoea, particularly for children, so fluid replenishment is the number one treatment. Weak black tea with a little sugar, soda water, or soft drinks allowed to go flat and diluted 50% with water are all good. In instances of severe diarrhoea, a rehydrating solution is necessary to replace minerals and salts. You should stick to a bland diet as you recover.

Lomotil or Imodium can be used to bring relief from the symptoms, although they do not actually cure the problem. Only use these drugs if absolutely necessary – eg, if you *must* travel. For children, Imodium is preferable, but do not use these drugs if the patient has a high fever or is severely dehydrated.

Antibiotics can be very successful in the treatment of severe diarrhoea, especially if it is accompanied by nausea, vomiting, stomach cramps or mild fever. Ampicillin, a broad spectrum penicillin, is recommended. Two capsules of 250 mg each taken four times a day is the recommended dose for an adult. Children aged between eight and 12 years should have half the adult dose; younger children should have half a capsule four times a day. Note that if the patient is allergic to penicillin, ampicillin should not be administered.

Three days of treatment should be sufficient and an improvement should occur within 24 hours.

Giardia The intestinal parasite that causes giardia is present in contaminated water. The symptoms are stomach cramps, nausea, a bloated stomach, watery, foul-smelling diarrhoea and frequent gas. Giardia can appear several weeks after you have been exposed to the parasite. The symptoms may disappear for a few days and then return; this can go on for several weeks. Metronidazole, known as Flagyl, is the recommended drug, but it should only be taken under medical supervision. Antibiotics are of no use.

Dysentery This serious illness is caused by contaminated food or water and is characterised by severe diarrhoea, often with blood or mucus in the stool. There are two kinds of dysentery. Bacillary dysentery is characterised by a high fever and rapid development; headache, vomiting and stomach pains are also symptoms. It usually does not last longer than a week, but it is highly contagious.

Amoebic dysentery is more gradual in developing, has no fever or vomiting but is a more serious illness. A stool test is necessary to diagnose which kind of dysentery you have, so you should seek medical help urgently. In case of an emergency, note that tetracycline is the prescribed treatment for bacillary dysentery, metronidazole for amoebic dysentery.

With tetracycline, the recommended adult dosage is one 250 mg capsule four times a day. Children aged between eight and 12 years should have half the adult dose; the dosage for younger children is a third the adult dose. It's important to remember that tetracycline should be given to young children only if it's absolutely necessary and only for a short period; pregnant women should not take it after the 4th month of pregnancy.

With metronidazole, the recommended adult dosage is one 750 to 800-mg capsule three times daily for five days. For children aged between eight and 12 years, administer half the adult dose; the dosage for younger children is a third the adult dose.

Viral Gastroenteritis This is caused not by bacteria but, as the name suggests, by a virus. It is characterised by diarrhoea, stomach cramps and sometimes by vomiting and/or a slight fever. All you can do is rest and drink lots of fluids.

Hepatitis Hepatitis A is the more common form of this disease and is commonly spread by contaminated food or water. The first symptoms are fever, chills, headache, fatigue, feelings of weakness and aches and pains. This is followed by loss of appetite, nausea, vomiting, abdominal pain, dark urine, light-coloured faeces and jaundiced skin; the whites of the eyes may also turn yellow.

In some cases, there may just be a feeling of being unwell or tired, accompanied by loss of appetite, aches and pains and the jaundiced effect. You should seek medical advice, but in general there is not much you can do apart from resting, drinking lots of fluids, eating lightly and avoiding fatty foods. People who have had hepatitis must forgo alcohol for six months after the illness,

as hepatitis attacks the liver and it needs that amount of time to recover.

Hepatitis B, which used to be called serum hepatitis, is spread through sexual contact or through skin penetration – it can be transmitted via dirty needles or blood transfusions. The symptoms and treatment of type B are much the same as for type A, but gamma globulin as a prophylactic is only effective against type A.

Typhoid Typhoid fever is another gut infection that travels the faecal-oral route – ie, contaminated water and food are responsible. Vaccination against typhoid is not totally effective and it is one of the most dangerous infections, so medical help must be sought.

Worms These parasites are most common in rural, tropical areas. They can be present on unwashed vegetables or in undercooked meat, and you can pick them up through your skin by walking in bare feet. Infestations may not show up for some time, and although they are generally not serious, if left untreated, they can cause severe health problems. A stool test is necessary to pinpoint the problem and medication is often available over the counter.

Diseases Spread by People & Animals

Tetanus This potentially fatal disease is found in undeveloped tropical areas. It is difficult to treat but is preventable with immunisation. Tetanus occurs when a wound becomes infected by a germ which lives in the faeces of animals or people, so clean all cuts, punctures or animal bites.

Rabies Rabies is caused by a bite or scratch from an infected animal – dogs and monkeys are common carriers. Any bite, scratch or even lick from a mammal should be cleaned immediately and thoroughly. Scrub with soap and running water, and then clean the area with an alcohol solution. If there is any possibility that the animal is infected, medical help should be sought immediately.

Other Diseases If current epidemics of

meningococcal meningitis have been reported, vaccination should be considered. Good protection is given for one year. Note that the disease has been reported in Vietnam. Tuberculosis is not a serious risk to travellers, although children under 12 should be vaccinated.

Insect-Borne Diseases

Malaria Malarial mosquitoes are rife in Cambodia, particularly along the Thai border and in the remote northern regions. Not only has Chloroquine resistance been reported but also resistance to other antimalarials. Malaria is a very serious disease which is spread by mosquito bites and it is extremely important to take malarial prophylactics while in Cambodia. Symptoms include headaches, fever, chills and sweating which may subside and recur. Without proper treatment, malaria can develop more serious, potentially fatal effects.

Antimalarial drugs do not actually prevent the disease but do suppress its symptoms. Chloroquine is the most usual malarial prophylactic; a tablet is taken once a week for two weeks prior to arrival in the infected area and six weeks after you leave it. Since Chloroquine resistance is widespread in Cambodia, you should instead take a weekly dose of Larium or Maloprim or a daily dose of Proguanil.

Chloroquine is quite safe for general use, side effects are minimal and it can be taken by pregnant women. Maloprim can have rare but serious side effects if the weekly dose is exceeded, and some doctors recommend a check-up after six months of continuous use. Fansidar, once a Chloroquine alternative, is no longer recommended as a prophylactic, as it can have dangerous side effects, but it may still be recommended as a treatment for malaria. Chloroquine is also used for malaria treatment but in greater doses than for prophylaxis.

Mosquitoes appear after dusk. Avoiding bites by covering bare skin and using an insect repellent will further reduce the risk of catching malaria. Insect screens on windows and mosquito nets on beds offer protection, as does burning a mosquito coil. Mosquitoes may be attracted by perfume, aftershave or certain colours. The risk of infection is higher in rural areas and during the wet season.

Dengue Fever There is no prophylactic available for this mosquito-spread disease; the main preventative measure is to avoid mosquito bites. A sudden onset of fever, headaches and severe joint and muscle pains are the first signs before a rash starts on the trunk of the body and spreads to the limbs and face. After a few more days, the fever will subside and recovery will begin. Serious complications are not common.

Cuts, Bites & Stings

Cuts & Scratches Skin punctures can easily become infected in hot climates and may be difficult to heal. Treat any cut with an antiseptic solution and mercurochrome. Where possible avoid bandages and Band-aids, which can keep wounds wet.

Snakes To minimise your chances of being bitten, always wear boots, socks and long trousers when walking through undergrowth where snakes may be present. Don't put your hands into holes and crevices. Snake bites do not cause instantaneous death; keep the victim calm and still, wrap the bitten limb tightly, as you would for a sprained ankle, and then attach a splint to immobilise it. Then seek medical help, if possible with the dead snake for identification. Don't attempt to catch the snake if there is even a remote possibility of being bitten again. Tourniquets and the sucking out of the poison are comprehensively discredited as a means of treatment now.

Bedbugs Bedbugs live in various places, but particularly in dirty mattresses and bedding. Spots of blood on bedclothes or on the wall around the bed can be read as a suggestion to find another hotel. Bedbugs leave bites in neat rows. Calamine lotion may help to relieve the itchiness.

Leeches & Ticks

Leeches may be present in damp rainforest conditions; they attach themselves to your skin to suck your blood. Salt or a lighted cigarette end will make them fall off. Do not pull them off, as the bite is then more likely to become infected. An insect repellent may keep them away. Vaseline, alcohol or oil will persuade a tick to let go.

Traditional Medicine

Traditional medicine is widely practised in Cambodia, in part because Western medical care is largely unavailable (the Khmer Rouge killed almost all of the country's doctors who did not flee abroad). Some traditional treatments (eg the use of some herbs) appear to work, but others, such as that based on the belief that paraplegics can be cured by suspending them over a fire, produce catastrophic results.

The vertical red marks often visible on the necks and torsos of both male and female Cambodians are made by rubbing the skin very hard with coins. This treatment is supposed to dilate the blood vessels and is said to be good for anyone who is feeling weak or ill.

Headaches are treated by applying suction cups to the forehead and face. These have the same effect on blood circulation as leeches – namely, to draw blood to the point of suction.

DANGERS & ANNOYANCES
Security

Until the civil war ends completely, travel outside areas under firm government control (of which there are few) will carry with it a certain degree of risk, especially in the evening and after dark. Although it is true that since 1979 not a single Western journalist or aid worker has been wounded or killed in the fighting, maintaining that perfect record depends on continued good judgement on the part of the thousands of illiterate, nervous and heavily armed teenagers fighting on both sides. While no one in Phnom Penh (including the people who issue travel permits) really knows what is going on out in the provinces, the latest rumours are available from long-term foreign-aid workers, many of whom work in rural areas despite the variable security conditions, and government officials.

While Western aid teams regularly travel (in well-marked vehicles) to areas with frequent rebel activity, Russians, Germans and Czechs working in Cambodia are confined to Phnom Penh, apparently not without good reason.

Undetonated Mines, Mortars & Bombs

Never, ever touch any rockets, artillery shells, mortars, mines, bombs or other war material you may come across. In Vietnam most of this sort of stuff is 15 or more years old, but in Cambodia it may have landed there or been laid as recently as the previous night. In fact, a favourite tactic of the Khmer Rouge has been to lay mines along roads and in rice fields in an effort to maim and kill civilians, thus – so their twisted logic concludes – furthering the rebel cause by demoralising the government. The only concrete results of this policy are the many limbless people you see all over Cambodia. The most heavily mined part of the country is along the Thai border. In short: *do not* stray from well-marked paths under any circumstances, even around the monuments of Angkor.

My own experience illustrates some of the dangers travellers to Cambodia in the 1990s may encounter: having received all necessary official authorisations, my guide, a companion and I went to explore Angkor's Preah Khan Temple. After we'd been there for a while, merrily making our way among the galleries, two breathless soldiers ran up and informed our horrified guide (a man with a dozen children) that the night before, government sappers had booby-trapped the area with antipersonnel mines rigged to filament trip wires. Two years later, in 1992, the Preah Khan Temple is open without requiring any additional official permission.

What to do about the mines is a topic of considerable interest in Cambodia. An international aid group known as the Halo Trust is mapping the mine fields, so that the areas to steer clear of will at least be known. Suggested methods of clearing the mines include offering a bounty for each mine turned in, but this raises the spectre of even more injuries being caused and the possibility of mines being 'found' which have never been laid. Another suggestion is that demobilised soldiers from the central government and the guerrilla forces could be usefully employed to clear the mines. If the UN-brokered peace really does spread, Cambodia will soon have a large contingent of unemployed ex-soldiers and if anybody knows where the mines are and how to deal with them they should.

Snakes

Visitors to Angkor and other overgrown archaeological sites should beware of snakes, including the small but deadly light-green Hanuman snake.

Theft & Street Crime

In Phnom Penh, war cripples, who receive almost no help from the government, are organised into gangs whose members hobble from store to store extorting money from the owners. Automobiles and buses are sometimes held up at gunpoint along Cambodia's highways, but foreigners are almost never involved in such incidents.

Traffic Accidents

Cambodia appears to have some of the most lethal drivers I have ever encountered. Every week I was in Cambodia I saw several serious traffic accidents involving huge trucks and either pedestrians or cyclists. The tendency to recklessness on the part of Cambodia's unschooled drivers is exacerbated by their natural inclination to drive through congested areas as quickly as possible.

Visitors should remember that ambulance and rescue services are almost non-existent outside of Phnom Penh. It will probably take many hours for a person injured in a rural area to be transported to a hospital, where only the most basic treatment may be available.

ACCOMMODATION

Phnom Penh and Siem Reap (near Angkor) have a very limited number of 1 or 2-star hotel rooms but many new or renovated hotels are under construction, including several more luxurious places. With tourism growing rapidly, prices are already starting to escalate and accommodation shortages have developed despite the growing number of hotels. Most provincial capitals have some sort of very basic hotel or official guest house.

FOOD

Cambodian food is closely related to the cuisines of neighbouring Thailand and Laos and, to a lesser extent, Vietnam, but there are some distinct local dishes. In the growing number of restaurants in Phnom Penh and Siem Reap, you will find excellent Chinese and Vietnamese dishes but it's the local dishes which are often the best prepared and most interesting. Rice is the principal staple and the Battambang Region is the country's rice bowl. Most Cambodian dishes are cooked in a wok, known locally as a *chhnang khteak*.

A Cambodian meal almost always includes a soup or *samla* dish but this is eaten at the same time as the other courses, not as a separate starter. *Samla machou banle* is a popular fish soup with a sour flavour rather like the sour-hot dishes of neighbouring Thailand. Other soups include *samla chapek* (ginger-flavoured pork soup) or *samlo machou bangkang* (a prawn soup closely related to the popular Thai *tom yam)*.

Much of the fish eaten in Cambodia is freshwater, from the great Tonlé Sap Lake or from the Mekong River. *Trey Aing*, or grilled fish, is a Cambodian speciality (*aing* means grilled in Khmer and can be applied to many dishes). Traditionally, the fish is eaten in pieces which are wrapped in lettuce or spinach leaves and dipped into a fish sauce known as *tuk trey*, a close relative of Vietnam's *nam pla* or *nuoc mam* but with the addition of ground peanuts. *Trey noueng phkea* is fish stuffed with small dried prawns, *trey chorm hoy* is steamed whole fish, and

Signs (TW)

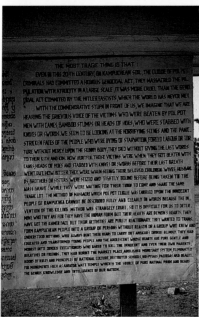

Top: Tuol Sleng map (TW)
Left: Choeung Ek (TW)
Right: Choeung Ek Memorial Stupa (TW)

Top: Fishing on the Mekong River (TW)
Left: Mekong River (TW)
Right: Fishermen, Mekong River (TW)

Top: Trunk of live sugar palm shot clear through, Tonlé Bati (DR)
Bottom: Relief of Preah Vesandar story, Ta Prohm Temple, Tonlé Bati (DR)

trey chean noeung spei is fried fish served with vegetables.

Cambodian 'salad' dishes are also popular and delicious although quite different from the Western idea of a cold salad. *Phlea sach ko* is a beef and vegetable salad, flavoured with coriander, mint leaves and lemon grass. These three herbs find their way into the flavouring of many Cambodian dishes.

Khao phoune is one of the most common Cambodian dishes and is found everywhere from street stalls to homes. Closely related to Malaysia's *laksa* dishes, the fine rice noodles are prepared in a sauce enriched with coconut milk.

As in Vietnam, the French influence is most clearly seen in the delicious bread, freshly baked every day. In the markets you may come across some less appetising local specialities, such as turtles baked in their shells. Frogs' legs are also popular.

At weddings and other festivities sweet

specialities like *ansam chruk*, sticky rice balls stuffed with banana, are served. *Nom bat* and *nom kom* are other sticky rice cakes or there is *phleay*, a pastry and palm sugar concoction which is fried and rolled in grated coconut. The large fruit known as jackfruit is used to make a pudding known as *sangkcha khnor*.

DRINKS

Soda water with lemon is called *soda kroch chhmar*; the custom here seems to be to let customers squeeze their own lemons. Cans of soft drinks and beer are readily available in Cambodia at around US$1. Beer is principally imported from Singapore and is clearly a great waste of precious foreign exchange. In 1992, however, an Australian brewing company is reintroducing Bayon and Angkor beer to the local market from their brewery in Kompong Som. They will also be bottling international brands of soft drinks.

In Phnom Penh, ice (*tuk kak*) is produced by a factory that apparently uses treated water of some sort. Drinking tap water is to be avoided, especially in the provinces.

Adulterated Soft Drinks

Beware: some of the flavoured soda sold in bottles by kerbside vendors has been made cheaply by a process that renders the resultant product toxic enough to cause headaches and stomach upsets.

THINGS TO BUY

The checked cotton scarves everyone wears on their heads, around their necks or, if bathing, around their midriffs, are known as *kramas*. Fancier coloured versions are made of silk or a silk-cotton blend. Some of the finest cotton kramas come from the Kompong Cham area.

For information on where in Phnom Penh to find antiques, silver items, jewellery, gems, colourful cloth for sarongs and *hols* (variegated silk shirts), wood carvings, papier-mâché masks, stone copies of ancient Khmer art, brass figurines and oil paintings, see Things to Buy in the Phnom Penh chapter.

Getting There & Away

TOURS

Many visitors to Cambodia come on organised tours because making bookings and arranging visas independently can be time consuming. The majority of independent visitors to Cambodia come in via Saigon in Vietnam although more travellers are now entering on the more expensive daily flights from Bangkok.

From Australia

Orbitours (☎ (02) 221 7322; fax (02) 221 7425), GPO Box 3309, Sydney 2000, Australia, is a major tour operator for English-speaking visitors from other countries as well as Australia. They operate tours ex-Bangkok which cost US$1320 or A$1737 for four days or US$1790 or A$2355 for seven days. These include the Bangkok-Phnom Penh-Bangkok and Phnom Penh-Siem Reap (Angkor)-Phnom Penh flights, accommodation, tours and meals while at Angkor. They also have longer tours which combine Cambodia with the other countries in Indochina.

From the UK

Regent Holidays (UK) Ltd (☎ (0272) 211711, fax (0272) 254866), 13 Small St, Bristol BS1 1DE is a major operator from the UK.

From North America

The *US Trading with the Enemy Act* (since Phnom Penh was the 'enemy' this made the Khmer Rouge the ally) has hampered Americans wanting to visit Cambodia, but with the UN now active in the country the situation will become easier. North American agents to contact include:

California
    Budgetours International, 8907 Westminster Ave, Garden Grove, CA 92644 (☎ (714) 221-6539, 637-8229, 895-2528)
    Diva Worldwide, 123 Townsend St, Suite 245, San Francisco, CA 94107 (☎ (415) 777 5351; fax (415) 334 6365)
    Tour Connections, 8907 Westminster Ave, Garden Grove, CA 92644 (☎ (213) 465-7315, (714) 895-2839)
New York
    Mekong Travel, 151 First Ave, Suite 172, New York, NY 10003 (☎ (212) 420-1586)
Ontario
    Angkor Wat Adventures, 653 Mt Pleasant Rd, Toronto, Ontario M4S 2N2 (☎ (416) 482-1223; fax (416) 486-4001)
Pennsylvania
    US-Indochina Reconciliation Project, 5808 Green St, Philadelphia, PA 19144 (☎ (215) 848-4200)

បណ្ណធ្វើឱ្យយន្តហោះ

BOARDINGPASS

រាជសីមាកម្ពុជា

KAMPUCHEA AIR LINES

ភ្នំពេញ	ក្រោះពៅ	គ័ប៊ាន់យុរ្យបិ
FLTNO	DESTINATION	CABINBAG

Quebec

Club Voyages Berri, 1650 Berri, Suite 8, Montreal, Quebec H2L 4E6 (☎ (514) 982-6168/9; fax (514) 982-0820)

New Asia Tours (Tour Nouvelle Asie), 1063 Blvd St Laurent, Montreal, Quebec H2Z 1J6 (☎ (514) 874-0266; fax (514) 874- 0251)

Que Viet Tours, 1063 Blvd St Laurent, Montreal, Quebec H2Z 1J6; (☎ (514) 393-3211; fax (514) 874-0251)

From Thailand

In Bangkok, Diethelm Travel is a major operator in tours to Indochina. It is usually somewhat more expensive than other Bangkok operators. The four-day trip to Phnom Penh and Angkor costs US$1350 each for a minimum of two people and includes the Bangkok-Phnom Penh-Bangkok flight. They also have five-day trips including Vientiane in Laos and eight-day trips including Vientiane and Ho Chi Minh City in Vietnam.

Many other smaller operators in Bangkok will also arrange travel to Cambodia with typical costs around US$350 to US$450 for a three-day/two-night stay in Phnom Penh including accommodation, transfers and visa fee but not including the Bangkok-Phnom Penh-Bangkok airfare. You need to allow about a week for the visa application. Some of these agents will arrange just your air travel and visa without obliging you to book tours and accommodation. Agents in the popular Khao San Rd travellers' enclave in Bangkok, like Vista Travel, are good at this. To phone or fax Bangkok from abroad, dial the country code (66) and the Bangkok code (2). Agents to try include:

Air People Tour & Travel Co Ltd

2nd floor, Regent House Building, 183 Rajdamri Rd, Bangkok 10500 (☎ 254-3921-5; fax 255-3750)

Diethelm Travel

Kian Gwan Building II, 140/1 Wireless Rd, Bangkok 10500 (☎ 255- 9150/60/70; fax 256-0248/9).

Exotissimo Travel (Bolsa Travelmart)

21/17 Sukhumvit Soi 4, Bangkok 10110 (☎ 253-5240/1, 255-2747; fax 254-7683)

755 Silom Rd, Bangkok 10500 (☎ 235-9196; fax 233-4885)

Lam Son International Ltd

23/1 Sukhumvit Soi 4 (Soi Nana Tai), Bangkok 10110 (☎ 255-6692-5, 252-2340; fax 255-8859)

Namthai Travel

Bangkok (☎ 215-9003/10, 215-7339; fax 215-6240)

Red Carpet Service & Tour

459 New Rama 6 Rd, Phayathai, Bangkok 10400 (☎ 215-9951, 215-3331; fax 215-3331)

Thaninee Trading Company

1131/343 Terddumri Rd, Dusit, Bangkok 10300 (☎ 243-1794, 243-2601, 243-3245; fax 243-0676)

Tri Virgo International Travel

377 Charoen Krung Rd, Bangkok 10500 (☎ 234-4642; fax 233-4776)

Viet Tour Holidays (The Crescendo Co Ltd)

1717 Lard-Prao Rd, Samsennok, Huay-Kwang, Bangkok 10310 (☎ 511- 3272; fax 511-3357)

Vikamla Tours (same office as Lam Son International) Room 401, Nana Condo, 23/11 Sukhumvit Soi 4 (Soi Nana Tai), Bangkok 10110 (☎ 252-2340, 255-8859)

Vista Travel Ltd

24/4 Khao San Rd, Banglumphoo, Bangkok (☎ 280-0348, 281-0786; fax 280-0348)

From Other Countries

To organise tours in Cambodia from abroad, contact the following agents:

France

Hit Voyages, 21 Rue des Bernardins, 75005 Paris (☎ 43 54 17 17)

Pacific Holidays, 34 Ave du Général Leclerc, 75014 Paris (☎ 45 41 52 58)

International Tourisme, 26 Blvd St Marcel, 75005 Paris (☎ 45 87 07 70)

Germany

Indoculture Tours (Indoculture Reisedienst GmbH), Bismarckplatz 1 D-7000 Stuttgart 1 (☎ 0711/61 7057-58)

Saratours, Sallstrasse 21 D-3000, Hanover 1 (☎ 0511-282353)

Hong Kong

Chu & Associates, Unit E, 5/F, 8 Thomson Rd, Hong Kong (☎ 5-278828/41)

Vietnam Tours & Trading Company, Room 302, Loader Commercial Building, 54 Hillwood Rd, TST (☎ 3-682493, 3-676663)

Travel Services (HK) Ltd, Metropole Building, 57 Peking Rd, Tsim Tsa Tsui, Kowloon (☎ 674127)

Phoenix Services Agency, Room B, 6/F, Milton Mansion, 96 Nathan Rd, Kowloon (☎ 7-227378; telex 3167 PHNXHK)

New Zealand
    Destinations, 2nd floor, Premier Building, 4
    Durham St, Auckland (☎ (09) 390-464)
Switzerland
    Exotissimo, 8 Ave du Mail, 1205 Geneva (☎ 022-
    81.21.66; telex 421358 EXOT CH; fax 022-81
    21 71)
    Artou, 8 Rue de Rive, 1204 Geneva
    Nayak, Steinengrabes 42, CH-4001 Basel
    (☎ 061-224343)

AIR

International connections with Cambodia are rapidly improving and once full diplomatic relations with neighbouring countries have been re-established flights will soon follow. Recent construction at Phnom Penh's Pochentong Airport will allow it to handle large jet aircraft. Meanwhile, you can fly to Phnom Penh from Bangkok or Singapore and there are strong rumours that flights will soon commence between Bangkok and Siem Reap.

Phnom Penh is also served by flights operated by Kampuchean Airlines (the national carrier), Aeroflot, Lao Aviation and Vietnam Airlines. The flight possibilities are outlined in the following sections.

Bangkok

Bangkok Airways now has two flights a day between Bangkok and Phnom Penh using 54-seat Dash 8 aircraft. The return fare is a hefty US$500 and the flight takes 1¾ hours. Officially these are charter flights and reservations are made through Transindo Ltd (☎ (66-2) 287-3241-4), 9/F Thasos Building, Chand Rd, Bangkok 10120. In practice, the flights operate just like scheduled services. Siam-Kampuchea Air or SK Air is also operating Bangkok-Phnom Penh using the same F28 aircraft as Phnom Penh Airways (see the following Singapore section).

Singapore & Hong Kong

Phnom Penh Airways operates a weekly flight to Phnom Penh on Tuesdays using chartered 100-seat F28 jet aircraft of the Indonesian airline Pelita. The flight costs US$300 one-way from Singapore (US$260 from Phnom Penh) and takes two hours.

Book through Airtrust (Singapore) Pty Ltd (☎ (65) 280-7133), 3 New Industrial Rd, Singapore 1953. Airtrust also has an office in Hong Kong (☎ (852) 549 4484) at Room 902, Wing Yue Building, 60-64 Des Voeux Rd West, Central.

Kuala Lumpur

Malaysian Airways (MAS) have reportedly commenced twice weekly direct flights between Kuala Lumpur and Phnom Penh.

Ho Chi Minh City (Saigon)

There are flights on most Mondays, Tuesdays, Wednesdays and Thursdays with Vietnam Airlines or Kampuchean Airlines. The flights cost US$46 one-way and take 40 minutes by Antonov An24.

Hanoi

There are flights every Tuesday or Wednesday with Vietnam Airlines or Kampuchean Airlines. The flights cost US$175 one-way and take three hours by An24 or 1½ hours by Tupolev Tu134).

Vientiane

There are flights with Lao Aviation or Kampuchean Airlines to/from Vientiane (US$120 each way; 3½ hours) via Pakse, Laos (US$50 one-way) on Wednesdays and Fridays.

Moscow

Aeroflot operates via Bombay three or four times a month.

LEAVING CAMBODIA

Flights originating in the carrier's country of origin usually depart in the morning and make the return flight in the afternoon. There is a US$5 airport departure tax on international flights.

Most flights into and out of Cambodia are booked out well in advance, often by important people who put their names on the reservation lists on the off chance that they might like to fly that day. At 4 pm on the afternoon before departure, seats often open up for people without reservations. Check with the Kampuchean Airlines Booking Office in Phnom Penh for details.

When international flights depart from Phnom Penh things can get a little disorganised, although the chaos is usually handled with grace. It's wise to arrive at the airport about two hours before departure time; few of the staff speak English or French. Checked baggage is sometimes, but certainly not always, weighed carefully. The official limit is 20 kg on international flights but only 10 kg for domestic flights.

Kampuchean Airlines' fleet consists of Tupolev Tu134 jets and Antonov An24s turboprops along with a number of Russian helicopters. Many of the pilots and mechanics are also Russian. Don't be alarmed if the ventilation system suddenly begins pouring clouds of vapour into the cabin – this is completely normal on many Russian aircraft. Don't be surprised if your seat doesn't come equipped with seat belts either, as this is also not unusual.

OVERLAND
From Vietnam
The drive from Saigon to Phnom Penh via Moc Bai (on the border of Vietnam's Tay Ninh Province and Cambodia's Svay Rieng Province) takes about 6½ hours by car and between eight and 10 hours by bus, including a wait of up to two hours for the ferry across the Mekong at Neak Luong. The border crossing at Moc Bai, which is five km east of the Cambodian town of Bavet, is open daily from 6.30 am to 6 pm; snacks are available on the Vietnamese side.

When crossing into Cambodia, officials on the Vietnamese side collect passports and hold them for up to an hour. Bus passengers have their passports returned as they reboard the bus before crossing the frontier. Remember that Vietnamese visas list the ports of entry and exit you are allowed to use; changes must be made by the Foreign Ministry.

In Saigon, buses to Phnom Penh leave early each morning from Boi Xe 1A (☎ 93754) at 155 Nguyen Hue Blvd, which is almost next door to the Rex Hotel. The trip costs less than US$5. In Phnom Penh, daily buses to Saigon depart at 6 am from an office (☎ 2.3139) at the south-western corner of 211 St and Ok Nga Sou St (182 St). The office is open from 7 to 11 am and from 2 to 7 pm. It's also possible to rent a car and driver in Saigon for the trip to Phnom Penh.

From Laos
Cambodia's National Route 7 enters Lao territory about 50 km north of Stung Treng; north of the border, the road follows the eastern bank of the Mekong. At present, there is no land link between Stung Treng and Phnom Penh.

From Thailand
The Cambodians have plans to open their frontier with Thailand to travellers as soon as the Thais agree (and the region is under government control). Before the war, Cambodia's north-western train line linked Phnom Penh with the towns of Poipet (Poay Pet) and Aranyaprathet on the border of Thailand and Cambodia, whence connecting train service to Bangkok was available. There are plans to resume the Phnom Penh-Bangkok service as soon as the political and military situation permits.

The main road between Bangkok and Phnom Penh also crosses the Thai-Cambodian border at Poipet. Siem Reap, the town for Angkor Wat, is only 150 km from the Thai border at Poipet. In mid-1992 Thai and UN forces were working on clearing the road.

For more information on Cambodia's rail and road systems, see the Getting Around chapter.

SEA
Cambodia's only maritime port is Kompong Som (formerly Sihanoukville), which was built during the late 1950s. Policies on the arrival of tourists by sea have yet to be drafted by the government.

Getting Around

It is a good idea to carry a compass around with you – outside Phnom Penh, street names and numbers simply do not exist.

AIR

The regularly scheduled domestic air routes which link the capital with Angkor (Siem Reap) and the northern town of Stung Treng have recently been supplemented with flights to Battambang. There are two flights from Phnom Penh to Siem Reap (US$43 each way) and vice versa every day. Some days there are even more. Flights between Phnom Penh and Stung Treng (US$45 each way) or Phnom Penh and Battambang (also US$45 each way) are less frequent.

Depending on demand (especially from official delegations), special flights are sometimes added to:

Kampot	(US$23)
Koh Kong	(US$45)
Kompong Cham	(US$14)
Kompong Chhnang	(US$14)
Kompong Som	(US$40)
Kompong Thom	(US$23)
Kratie	(US$30)
Mondulkiri	(US$50)
Preah Vihear	(US$45)
Pursat	(US$45)
Ratanakiri	(US$60)
Sisophon	(US$55)
Svay Rieng	(US$23)
Takeo	(US$11)

Unless another charter flight is scheduled a few days later, you'll have to choose between spending only a few hours at your destination and making your way back overland.

The baggage weight limit for domestic flights is only 10 kg per passenger but it's not always checked. Flights are usually well over-booked (you'll often see three people squeezed into every two seats with others sitting in the luggage compartment) so reservations – especially to and from Siem Reap – should be made as far in advance as possible. It may prove impossible to confirm your

Siem Reap-Phnom Penh reservation until you get to Siem Reap. The airport tax for domestic flights is US$2.50 each way (US$5 for a round trip) and is usually included in your ticket price.

Helicopter

If you've got lots of money or are on an expense account, you might consider chartering a Soviet-built helicopter for sightseeing or aerial photography. A round-trip excursion from Phnom Penh to Angkor for up to a dozen people costs US$6000.

BUS

At the time of writing, it was forbidden – not without reason, given the security situation – for foreigners to travel around Cambodia by bus. The various permits necessary to undertake any travel outside of Phnom Penh will not be issued for bus travel.

TRAIN

Cambodia's rail system consists of about 645 km of single-track metre-gauge lines. The 382 km north-western line, built before WW II, links Phnom Penh with Pursat (165 km from the capital), Battambang (274 km from the capital) and, in peacetime, Poipet (Poay Pet) on the Thai border. The 263 km south-western line, completed in 1969, connects the capital with Takeo (75 km from Phnom Penh), Kampot (160 km from the capital), Kep (get off at Damnak Chang Aeu) and the port of Kompong Som.

In recent years, Cambodia's rail system has suffered from frequent rebel sabotage. As a result, each train is equipped with a tin-roofed armoured carriage sporting a huge machine gun and gun ports in its half-height sides. In addition, the first two cars of the train are supposed to remain empty in order to detonate any mines placed on the track. Until recently, passage on these first carriages was free, and many peasants coming to the city to market their produce and buy goods to resell back home preferred to take their chances with Khmer Rouge mines rather than part with the fare. A severe shortage of rolling stock provides further encouragement for people to try their luck on the first two flatcars.

The duration of rail journeys in Cambodia is highly unpredictable. Because of sabotage and dilapidated equipment, the Phnom Penh-Battambang train must sometimes stop overnight en route at some safe government garrison, taking two or more days to travel a distance that under normal conditions can be covered in 12 hours.

BOAT

Cambodia's 1900 km of navigable waterways are an important element in the country's transportation system. Phnom Penh, which is some 320 km from the mouth of the Mekong, can be reached by oceangoing vessels with a draft of less than 3.3 metres. North of the capital, the Mekong is navigable as far north as Kratie; from September to January, boats can make it as far as Stung Treng. For information on ferry services to/from Phnom Penh, see the Getting There & Away section of the Phnom Penh chapter.

DRIVING

Cambodia's 15,000 km of roads, which include over 1800 bridges of more than seven metres in length, were designed by the French to link the agricultural hinterlands of colonial Cambodia with the port of Saigon. Because the road network was never intended to serve specifically Cambodian needs, huge areas in the north, north-east and south-west have been left almost completely without roads.

Even the small part of the network that was at one time surfaced (some 2500 km) has seriously deteriorated during the last two decades and today is only marginally serviceable – and virtually impassable to passenger cars. The rest of the country's roads, which were surfaced with crushed stone, gravel or laterite or were simply graded without being paved, are in even

worse shape. Because maintenance of all but the major highways is the responsibility of provincial governments, little repair work is being done. In addition, many of Cambodia's road bridges, including some of the largest and most important, have been destroyed, making land travel either very slow, with long waits at ferry crossings, or simply impossible.

The Road Network

Cambodia's major highways are conveniently numbered from one to seven. National Route 1 links Phnom Penh with Saigon via Svay Rieng and the Moc Bai border crossing, which is five km east of the Cambodian town of Bavet. National Route 2 heads south from the capital, passing through Takmau and Takeo on its way to Vietnam's An Giang Province and the city of Chau Doc. National Route 3 links the capital with the southern coastal city of Kampot. National Route 4 connects Phnom Penh and the country's only maritime port, Kompong Som, which is on the Gulf of Thailand, south-west of the capital.

National Route 5 heads north from Phnom Penh, circling around to the south of the Tonlé Sap and passing through Kompong Chhnang, Pursat, Battambang and Sisophon on its way north-westward to the Thai frontier. National Route 6 splits off from National Route 5 at the Prek Kdam Ferry over the Tonlé Sap River, heading northward and then north-westward on a route that goes to the north of the Tonlé Sap and passes through Kompong Thom, Siem Reap and Sisophon on its way to Thailand. National Route 7 splits from National Route 6 at Skun, heading eastward to Kompong Cham and eventually to Memot (Memut), Kratie, Stung Treng and the Lao border; the latter sections are currently impassable.

BICYCLE

When things quieten down, mountain bikes will be a superb way to get around on the country's potholed intercity roads.

HITCHING

There is a severe shortage of transport in Cambodia, so most trucks – the only vehicles other than large buses able to negotiate the country's dilapidated roads – are likely to be extremely crowded. Expect to pay for your ride. Don't even think of hitching until after the war is definitely over!

LOCAL TRANSPORT
Taxi

There are as yet no real taxis in Cambodia. If you need a car, you'll probably have to hire one on a daily basis – for US dollars cash – from one government ministry or another. The General Directorate of Tourism charges US$20/30 a day for cars without/with air-con. In Phnom Penh the Cambodiana Hotel has new cars at US$50 a day with driver.

Bicycle

Bicycles, called *kang* in street Khmer, are the best way to get to and from areas in the vicinity of where you're staying and are especially useful in Phnom Penh and around Angkor. For information on where to purchase one, see the Getting Around section in the Phnom Penh chapter. You can rent bicycles in Siem Reap to explore the Angkor ruins.

Cyclo

As in Vietnam and Laos, the samlor or cyclo is a quick, cheap way to get around Cambodia's urban areas. In Phnom Penh, cyclo drivers can either be flagged down on main thoroughfares or found hanging out around marketplaces and major hotels.

Remorque-Kang & Remorque-Moto

The *remorque-kang* is a trailer pulled by a bicycle; a trailer hitched to a motorbike is called a *remorque-moto*. Both are used to transport people and goods, especially in rural areas.

Phnom Penh

Phnom Penh, capital of Cambodia for much of the period since the mid-15th century (when Angkor was abandoned), is situated at Quatre Bras (literally, 'four arms' in French), the confluence of the Mekong River, the Bassac River and the Tonlé Sap River. Once considered the loveliest of the French-built cities of Indochina, its charm is still in evidence despite the violence and dilapidation of the last three decades. Indeed, the city has recently shown signs of renewed vitality.

The population of Phnom Penh was approximately 500,000 in 1970. After the spread of the Vietnam War to Cambodian territory, the city's population swelled with refugees, reaching about two million in early 1975. The Khmer Rouge took over the city on 17 April 1975 and immediately forced the entire population into the countryside as part of their radical social programme.

During the next four years, many tens of thousands of former Phnom Penhois — including the vast majority of the capital's educated people — were killed. Repopulation of the city began when the Vietnamese arrived in 1979. Many of Phnom Penh's 700,000 residents are peasants who have come to the city to improve their lot.

Orientation

Phnom Penh is a sprawling city and it can be a long way from one location to another. The city's most important north-south arteries are (from west to east): Achar Mean Blvd (where most of the hotels are), Tou Samouth Blvd, Lenin Blvd (in front of the Royal Palace) and, along the riverfront (which is also oriented roughly north to south), Quai Karl Marx. Forming two rough semicircles in the quadrant south-west of the Central Market are Sivutha Blvd (which intersects Tou Samouth Blvd at the Victory Monument) and Keo Mony Blvd (which intersects Tou Samouth Blvd at the former US Embassy).

The city's most important east-west thoroughfares are USSR Blvd (with its parallel side street, Soeung Ngoc Ming St), which intersects Achar Mean Blvd near the railway station, and Kampuchea-Vietnam Blvd (128 St), which heads due west from the Central Market. Before 1975, Kampuchea-Vietnam Blvd was known as Kampuchea Krom (Lower Cambodia) Blvd, a reference to the south-eastern portion of the Khmer Empire colonised and annexed by Vietnam a few centuries ago.

National Route 1 links the capital with Saigon, crossing the Bassac River over Monivong Bridge. National Route 2 goes south past Takmau to Takeo and An Giang Province in Vietnam. National Route 3, which heads west from the city, passes Pochentong Airport before linking up with south-westward bound National Route 4 to Kompong Som; National Route 3 continues southward to Takeo and Kampot. National Route 5 heads north from the city towards Udong, Kompong Cham, Kompong Thom, Siem Reap, Pursat, Battambang and Bangkok.

All of Phnom Penh's streets were renamed after 1979; major thoroughfares got real names while smaller streets were rather haphazardly assigned numbers. In most cases, odd-numbered streets run more or less north to south (usually parallel to Achar Mean Blvd), with the numbers rising in a semi-sequential order as you move from east to west. Even-numbered streets run in an east-west direction, rising semi-sequentially as you move from north to south. Several streets are misnumbered on the map of *Phnom Penh Ville* produced in the late 1980s by Phnom Penh Tourism.

Most buildings in the capital are marked with white-on-blue signs bearing two or three multidigit numbers. The number borne by every building on both sides of the street is the name of the street. Numerals common to several structures (usually housing 20 to 40 families) signify the number of the building's security and control group. Each

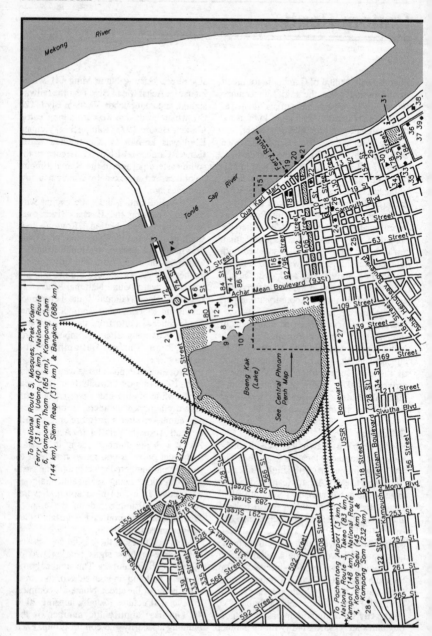

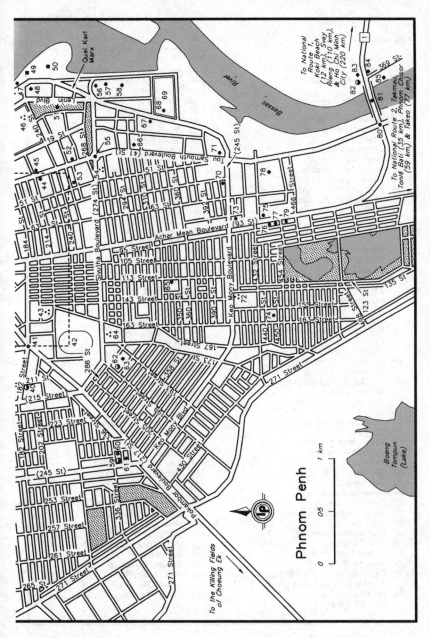

Phnom Penh

■ PLACES TO STAY

38	Hotel Renakse
49	Cambodiana Inn
50	Hotel Cambodiana

▼ PLACES TO EAT

4	Restaurant Kong Kea
9	Restaurant Raksmey Boeng Kak
10	Restaurant Thmey Boeng Kak
13	Restaurant Calmette
14	Restaurant Chez Lipp
15	Restaurant Tonlé Sap 2
20	Restaurant Tonlé Sap 1
30	No Problem Café

OTHER

1	Old Stadium (closed)
2	Fine Arts School (Music & Dance Faculties)
3	Chruoy Changvar Bridge (destroyed)
5	Former French Embassy
6	Bangkok Airways/ Transindo Office
7	Entrance to Boeng Kak Amusement Park
8	Boeng Kak Amusement Park
11	Entrance to Boeng Kak Amusement Park
12	Revolution (Calmette) Hospital
16	National Library
17	Wat Phnom
18	GPO
19	Psar Cha Ministry of Transport Ferry Landing
21	Psar Cha Municipal Ferry Landing
22	Old Market (Psar Char)
23	Railway Station
24	Customs House
25	Central Market
26	Former National Bank Site
27	Council of Ministers
28	Phnom Penh University
29	Wat Ounalom
31	Phnom Penh Tourism
32	National Museum
33	Fine Arts School (Main Campus) & École des Beaux-Arts Shop
34	Kampuchean Airlines Booking Office

35	'English Street'
36	Entrance to Royal Palace
37	Royal Palace
39	Entrance to Silver Pagoda
40	Bus to Ho Chi Minh City
41	Roundabout
42	National Sports Complex
43	Wat Sampao Meas
44	Soviet Cultural Centre
45	Ministry of the Interior
46	Silver Pagoda
47	Conference Hall
48	Foreign Ministry
51	Cambodia-Vietnam Monument
52	Czech Embassy
53	Australian Embassy
54	Wat Lang Ka
55	Victory Monument
56	Circus School
57	Exposition Hall
58	Bassac Theatre
59	Psar Dang Kor Bus Station
60	Dang Kor Market
61	Municipal Theatre
62	Olympic Intercity Bus Station
63	Olympic Market
64	Wat Moha Montrei
65	Tuol Sleng Museum
66	Prayuvong Buddha Factories
67	Russian Ambassador's Residence
68	Russian Embassy
69	Russian Compound
70	Lao Embassy
71	Former US Embassy
72	Wat Tuol Tom Pong
73	Vietnamese Embassy (Consular Section)
74	Tuol Tom Pong Market
75	Vietnamese Embassy
76	Hungarian Embassy
77	Polish Embassy
78	Cham Kar Mon Palace
79	Indian Embassy
80	Roundabout
81	Monivong Bridge
82	Psar Chbam Pao Local Bus Station
83	Chbam Pao Market
84	Psar Chbam Pao Shared-Taxi Station
85	Chbam Pao Ferry Landing

such group is overseen by someone living there who reports on local happenings to the police and acts as a liaison with the government (arranges permits for marriages, etc); such people are in an excellent position to extort money from their charges and often do so. The third number, different from that of the buildings to either side, is the street address. The letters 'EO' after a street address stand for *étage zéro*, which means 'ground floor' in French.

In the past, Tou Samouth Blvd was known as Blvd 9 October (under Lon Nol), Blvd Norodom (under Sihanouk) and Blvd Doudard de Lagrée (under the French). Achar Mean Blvd was previously called Blvd Monivong. During the colonial period, the area around the Royal Palace was known as the Cambodian Quarter, the neighbourhood around Wat Phnom was considered the European Quarter, and the Central Market was at the centre of the Chinese Quarter.

The city of Phnom Penh consists of four urban districts *(khand)* and three suburban districts *(srok)*.

Information

Tourist Office The head office of Phnom Penh Tourism (☎ 2.3949, 2.5349, 2.4059) is across from Wat Ounalom at the oblique intersection of Lenin Blvd and Quai Karl Marx; its two entrances are at 313 Quai Karl Marx and next to 2 Lenin Blvd. The office is officially open from 7 to 11 am and from 2 to 5 pm. Phnom Penh Tourism, which belongs to the Phnom Penh Municipality, restricts its activities to running three-day package tours that include a one-day visit to Angkor; these are marketed at great profit by Saigon Tourist in Ho Chi Minh City, leaving the Cambodians (and their guests) feeling fleeced.

General Directorate of Tourism Cambodia's newly established General Directorate of Tourism (in French, Direction Générale du Tourisme; ☎ 2.2107), sometimes referred to as Cambodia Tourism, is slated to become a fully fledged Ministry of Tourism in the near future. The directorate's

offices are in a white, two-storey building on the western side of Achar Mean Blvd at 232 St (across 232 St from 447 Achar Mean Blvd). The large slogan written in Khmer across the front of the structure reads 'Long Live the People's Revolutionary Party'. The General Directorate rents cars with and without air-conditioning and guides can also be hired. The General Directorate of Tourism is seeking foreign joint venture partners for projects to develop the tourism infrastructure.

Registration & Internal Travel Permits Permits to travel outside Phnom Penh are issued by the Ministry of the Interior, which is known for its hardline policies. The ministry offices are on the south-eastern corner of Tou Samouth Blvd and 214 St.

Useful Addresses The Ministry of Information & Culture (☎ 2.4769) is opposite 395 Achar Mean Blvd at the corner of 180 St (Croix Rouge St). It is officially open from 7 to 11 am and from 2.30 to 5.30 pm. The Press Office of the Foreign Ministry (☎ 2.2241) is based in the Foreign Ministry building on Quai Karl Marx. The Russian Cultural Centre (☎ 2.2581) is on the western side of Tou Samouth Blvd at 222 St (across the street from the Ministry of the Interior). The Customs House is on the western side of Tou Samouth Blvd just south of 118 St.

The Fine Arts School (École des Beaux-Arts) has faculties of music, classical Cambodian dance and the plastic arts; archaeology and architecture faculties are being added. The school, which has 800 secondary students and 150 university-level students, is divided between two campuses. The plastic arts, archaeology and architecture faculties are based on the main campus, which is at the back of the National Museum complex at the corner of 19 St and 184 St. Music and dance are taught at a facility on 70 St near the old stadium (now a military base).

Visa Extensions Visa extensions are granted by the Foreign Ministry (☎ 2.4641,

2.3241, 2.4441), whose offices are on the western side of Quai Karl Marx at 240 St (opposite the entrance to the Cambodiana Inn). There is an unofficial charge of US$10 to help grease the wheels of the bureaucracy, which may still take three or more days to get through all the paperwork necessary to approve prolonging your stay.

Money The Foreign Trade Bank (in French, Banque du Commerce Extérieur du Cambodge; formerly the National People's Bank; ☎ 2.4863) is at 26 Soeung Ngoc Ming St, which is on the corner of Achar Mean Blvd. The exchange window (bureau de change), which is on the right as you enter, is open Monday to Saturday from 7.30 to 11 am and from 2.30 to 5 pm.

Post & Telecommunications There is a Post & Telephone Office (PTT; ☎ 2.3324, 2.3509, 2.2909) across from the Hotel Monorom at the corner of Achar Mean Blvd and 126 St. International telephone services, which must be paid for in US dollars cash, are available from 7 am to noon and from 1 to 11 pm. The postal desk, where philatelic items are on sale, is open from 7 to 11.30 am and from 2 to 7.30 pm.

The GPO (☎ 2.4511) is on the western side of 13 St between 98 St and 102 St in a building built as a post office well before WW II. It is open from 6.30 am to 9 pm daily. The GPO offers postal services as well as domestic and international telegraph and telephone links.

Foreign Embassies While recognition was withheld from the Vietnamese-backed government of Cambodia, no Western nation had a diplomatic office in the country. That situation is rapidly changing and there will soon be more Western embassies to join the Australian mission, the first to be established in Phnom Penh. While they wait for buildings to be completed, many missions camp out at the Cambodiana Hotel and this is a good place to start any embassy search. Embassies include:

Australia
    11 254 St (just north of the Victory Monument) (☎ 2.6000/1)
Bulgaria
    227 Tou Samouth Blvd (☎ 2.3181/2)
Cuba
    30 214 St (☎ 2.4181/2, 2.4281/2, 2.4381/2)
Czechoslovakia
    Tou Samouth Blvd (between 256 St and 264 St; ☎ 2.3781, 2.3981, 2.5881, 2.5081)
Hungary
    773 Achar Mean Blvd (near 432 St; ☎ 2.2781/2)
India
    777 Achar Mean Blvd (at 458 St; ☎ 2.2981)
Laos
    111 214 St (☎ 2.5181/2)
Poland
    767 Achar Mean Blvd (between 432 St and 458 St; ☎ 2.3581/2)
Russia
    Lenin Blvd midway between 312 St and 394 St (☎ 2.2081/2)
Vietnam
    Achar Mean Blvd at 436 St, which is blocked off (☎ 2.5481/2, 2.5681). The consular section (☎ 2.3142) is on the eastern side of Achar Mean Blvd opposite number 749 (between 422 St and Keo Mony Blvd). It is open daily, except Saturday afternoons, Sundays and Vietnamese and Cambodian holidays, from 7.30 to 11 am and from 2 to 5 pm. Two photos are required for a visa, which takes at least two days to issue.

Bookshop The Librairie d'État, which is across the street from the Hotel Pailin at 224 Achar Mean Blvd, has a few posters and postcards but not much else. There are some book stalls in the Central Market. The shops in the Hotel Cambodiana have a very limited supply of books at very high prices. Young boys come around the popular restaurants in town selling books, maps and cards.

Maps Maps can be purchased from the booksellers at Tuol Tom Pong Market and from personable boys and young men who hang around restaurants frequented by foreigners. Some of their merchandise appears to have been appropriated from the Vietnamese army.

Emergency The best hospital in Phnom Penh is probably the Khmer-Soviet Hospital (Hôpital de l'Amitié Khmer-Soviétique), which is partly staffed by Russian physicians and has a limited supply of medicines. If you've got serious medical problems, the best advice is to hop on the next flight to Bangkok.

Royal Palace

Phnom Penh's Royal Palace (☎ 2.4958), which stands on the site of the former citadel, Banteay Kev (built in 1813), fronts Lenin Blvd between 184 St and 240 St. Since Sihanouk's return to Cambodia, visitors are only allowed to visit the palace's Silver Pagoda and its surrounding compound. Entry is not, at present, permitted to the rest of the palace complex. The Silver Pagoda is open to the public on Thursdays and Sundays (and daily except Mondays for official visitors) from 8 to 11 am and from 2 to 5 pm. The entry fee is US$2. There is an additional US$2 charge to bring a still camera into the complex; movie or video cameras cost US$5. Photography is not permitted inside the pagoda.

Chan Chaya Pavilion Performances of classical Cambodian dance were staged in Chan Chaya Pavilion, through which guests enter the grounds of the Royal Palace.

Throne Hall The Throne Hall (Palais du Trône; in Khmer, Preah Tineang Tevea Vinichhay), topped by a 59-metre-high tower inspired by the Bayon Temple at Angkor, was inaugurated in 1919 by King Sisowath; the present cement building replaced a vast wooden structure built on this site in 1869. The Throne Hall, which is 100 metres long and 30 metres wide, was used for coronations and ceremonies such as the presentation of credentials by diplomats. Some 80% of the items once displayed here were destroyed by the Khmer Rouge.

On the walls and ceiling of the Throne Hall are murals depicting the *Ramayana* epic. The group of chairs closest to the entrance was reserved for the use of high officials; the second ensemble of chairs was used by foreign ambassadors when they came to present their credentials. Between here and the king's pavilion are a gilded,

Palace Wat

mobile platform on which the king rode during royal processions, the queen's hammock (also used during processions), French-style thrones belonging to the king and queen (she sat to his left) and a sacred gong held by two elephant tusks. In front of the king's mobile platform are conch shells that are blown at coronations and bunched branches used by the police to keep order.

The king's pavilion, which was used only on coronation day, sits in the transept; overhead, four Garudas (mythical man-bird, the vehicle of Vishnu) provide symbolic protection. To either side are the queen's enclosed sedan chair and the king's open one. The nave to the right (north) was used to store the ashes of deceased members of the royal family before they were interred in stupas. The left-hand (southern) nave served as a chapel for the king. It was here that he consulted the royal fortune teller to determine the most auspicious dates for trips. Next comes a group of yellow upholstered chairs

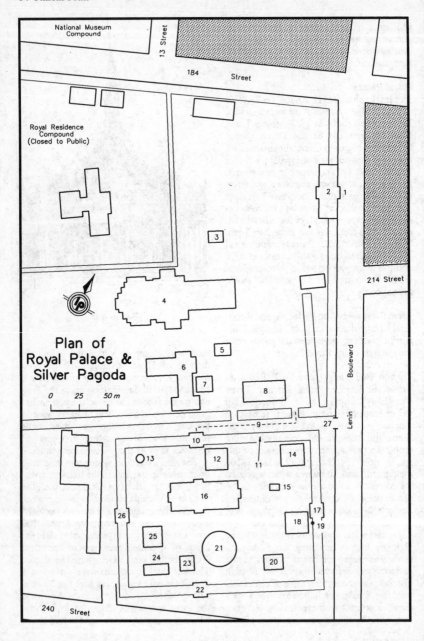

Top: Throne Hall of the Royal Palace, Phnom Penh (DR)
Left: Prince Sihanouk, Royal Palace, Phnom Penh (TW)
Right: Mondap, Silver Pagoda, Phnom Penh (TW)

    Top Left: Victory Monument, Phnom Penh (TW)
   Top Right: Cambodia-Vietnam Monument, Phnom Penh (TW)
Bottom Left: National Museum, Phnom Penh (DR)
Bottom Right: King Norodom Stupa (TW)

Top: Angkor Wat (TW)
Left: Angkor Wat (TW)
Right: Vishnu, Angkor Wat (TW)

Top Left: Angkor Wat at sunrise (TW)
Top Right: Angkor Wat (TW)
Bottom Left: Face tower, the Bayon (TW)
Bottom Right: Face tower, the Bayon (TW)

entrance to the Throne Hall is equipped with a dock from which the king could mount and dismount his elephant with ease and in comfort.

Silver Pagoda

The Silver Pagoda, so named because the floor is covered with over 5000 silver tiles weighing one kg each, is also known as Wat Preah Keo (Pagoda of the Emerald Buddha). It was constructed of wood in 1892 by King Norodom, who was apparently inspired by Bangkok's Wat Phra Keo, and rebuilt in 1962. The Silver Pagoda and its contents were preserved by the Khmer Rouge in order to demonstrate to the outside world their concern for the conservation of Cambodia's cultural riches. Although some 60% of the pagoda's contents were destroyed under Pol Pot, what's left is spectacular. This is one of the few places in all of Cambodia where objects embodying some of the brilliance and richness of Khmer civilisation can still be viewed.

The staircase leading up to the Silver Pagoda is made of Italian marble. Inside, the Emerald Buddha, said to be made of Baccarat crystal, sits on a gilt pedestal high atop the dais. In front of the dais stands a life-size gold Buddha decorated with 9584 diamonds, the largest of which weighs 25 carats. Created in the palace workshops during 1906 and 1907, the gold Buddha weighs some 90 kg. Directly in front of it, in a formica case, is a miniature silver-and-gold stupa containing a relic of the Buddha brought from Sri Lanka. To either side are an 80-kg bronze Buddha (to the left) and a silver Buddha (to the right). On the far right, figurines of solid gold tell the story of the Buddha.

Behind the dais are a standing marble Buddha from Myanmar and a litter, used by the king on coronation day, designed to be carried by 12 men; parts are made of 23 kg of gold. To either side are silver models of King Norodom's stupa and Wat Preah Keo's library. At the back of the hall is a case containing two gold Buddhas, each decorated with diamonds weighing up to 16

used by visiting heads of state during meetings with the king. The bed, flanked by two mirrors, was used by the king for naps, during which he was fanned by ladies of the court.

The queen's pavilion, which was used only during coronations, has three staircases; Brahmin officials participating in the ceremonies mounted from the sides, the queen herself from behind. Beyond is a large chamber flanked by the queen's bedroom (on the right) and the king's bedroom (on the left). For the seven days following the coronation ceremonies, the king and queen were required to sleep separately. During this period, they spent their nights here; then they moved to the royal residence.

Note that the structure just north of the

carats; the lower figure weighs 4.5 kg, the upper 1.5 kg.

Along the walls of the pagoda are examples of extraordinary Khmer artisanship, including bejewelled masks used in classical dance and dozens of solid and hollow gold Buddhas. The many precious gifts given to Cambodia's monarchs by foreign heads of state appear rather spiritless when displayed next to such diverse and exuberant Khmer art.

The epic of the *Ramayana* is depicted on a colossal mural, created around 1900, painted on the wall enclosing the pagoda compound; the story begins just south of the eastern gate. It is being restored with the assistance of Poland.

Other structures in the complex (listed clockwise from the North gate) include: the Mondap (library), which used to house richly illuminated sacred texts written on palm leaves; the stupa of King Norodom (reigned 1859 to 1904); an equestrian statue of King Norodom; the stupa of King Ang Duong (reigned 1845 to 1859); a pavilion housing a huge footprint of the Buddha; Phnom Mondap, an artificial hill at the top of which is a structure containing a bronze footprint of the Buddha from Sri Lanka; the stupa of one of Prince Sihanouk's daughters; a pavilion for celebrations held by the royal family; the stupa of Prince Sihanouk's father, King Norodom Suramarit (reigned 1955 to 1960); and a bell tower, whose bell is rung to order the gates to be opened or closed.

Museums

National Museum The National Museum of Khmer Art & Archaeology (also known as the Musée des Beaux-Arts and, during the French period, the Musée Albert Sarraut; ☎ 2.4369) is housed in an impressive red structure of traditional design (built 1917-20) just north of the Royal Palace on the western side of 13 St between 178 St and 184 St. It is open Tuesday to Sunday from 8 to 11 am and from 2 to 5 pm. Photography is prohibited inside. The Fine Arts School (École des Beaux-Arts) has its headquarters in a structure behind the main building.

The entrance fee for foreigners is US$2. Guides who speak French and English are available, and they may let you peruse an old copy of Henri Parmentier's comprehensive museum catalogue if you ask. The museum is undergoing a slow renovation to remove thousands of bats (and 15 years of accumulated bat droppings) from above the gallery's dropped ceiling, which is being taken out. During my visit, little bits of bat droppings kept floating down from the ceiling and swirling about in the air; every time I breathed in I could taste it on my tongue.

The National Museum contains many masterpieces of Khmer art, artisanship and sculpture dating from the pre-Angkor period of Funan and Chenla (4th to 9th centuries AD), the Indravarman period (9th and 10th centuries), the classical Angkor period (10th to 14th centuries) and the post-Angkor period (after the 14th century).

Tuol Sleng Museum In 1975, Tuol Svay Prey High School was taken over by Pol Pot's security forces and turned into a prison known as Security Prison 21 (S-21). It soon became the largest such centre of detention and torture in the country. Over 17,000 people held at S-21 were later taken to the extermination camp at Choeung Ek to be executed; detainees who died during torture were buried in mass graves on the prison grounds. S-21 has been turned into the Tuol Sleng Museum (☎ 2.4569), which serves as a testament to the crimes of the Khmer Rouge. The museum, whose entrance is on the western side of 113 St just north of 350 St, is open daily from 7 to 11.30 am and from 2 to 5.30 pm.

Like the Nazis, the Khmer Rouge were meticulous in keeping records of their barbarism. Each prisoner who passed through S-21 was photographed, sometimes both before and after being tortured. The museum displays include room after room in which such photographs of men, women and children cover the walls from floor to ceiling; virtually all the people pictured were later killed. You can tell in what year a picture was taken by the style of number board that appears on the prisoner's chest. Several foreigners from Australia, France and the USA were held here before being murdered. Their documents are on display.

As the Khmer Rouge 'revolution' reached ever greater heights of insanity, it began devouring its own children. Generations of torturers and executioners who worked here killed their predecessors and were in turn killed by those who took their places. During the first part of 1977, S-21 claimed an average of 100 victims a day.

When Phnom Penh was liberated by the Vietnamese army in early 1979, they found only seven prisoners alive at S-21. Fourteen others had been tortured to death as Vietnamese forces were closing in on the city. Photographs of their gruesome deaths are on display in the rooms where their decomposing corpses were found. Their graves are nearby in the courtyard.

There is something disconcerting about the way the present government in Phnom Penh is using Tuol Sleng Museum as an instrument of propaganda to boost its own legitimacy by focusing hatred on its predecessor. After all, most of the leaders of the Vietnamese-installed Phnom Penh government, including Hun Sen and Heng Samrin, were at one time Khmer Rouge officers themselves.

The Killing Fields of Choeung Ek Between 1975 and 1978, about 17,000 men, women, children and infants (including nine Westerners), detained and tortured at S-21 prison (now Tuol Sleng Museum), were transported to the extermination camp of Choeung Ek to be executed. They were bludgeoned to death to avoid wasting precious bullets.

The remains of 8985 people, many of whom were found bound and blindfolded, were exhumed in 1980 from mass graves in this one-time longan orchard; 43 of the 129 communal graves here have been left untouched. Fragments of human bone and bits of cloth are scattered around the disinterred pits. Over 8000 skulls, arranged by sex and age, are visible behind the clear glass

Skulls, Choeung Ek

panels of the Memorial Stupa, which was erected in 1988.

The Killing Fields of Choeung Ek are 15 km from downtown Phnom Penh. To get there, take Pokambor Blvd south-westward out of the city; the site is 8.5 km from the bridge near 271 St. A memorial ceremony is held annually at Choeung Ek on 9 May.

Military Museum The building housing the Military Museum, which is on the west side of Tou Samouth Blvd between 154 St and 172 St, is being used by the Cambodian army to train officers. It is closed to the public.

Wats & Mosques
Wat Phnom Set on top of a tree-covered knoll 27 metres high, Wat Phnom is visible from all over the city. According to legend, the first pagoda on this site, which is at the intersection of Tou Samouth Blvd and 96 St, was erected in 1373 to house four statues of the Buddha deposited here by the waters of the Mekong and discovered by a woman named Penh (thus the name Phnom Penh, 'the hill of Penh'). The main entrance to Wat .

Phnom is via the grand eastern staircase, which is guarded by lions and *naga* (snake) balustrades.

Today, many people come here to pray for good luck and success in school exams or business affairs. When a petitioner's wish is granted, he or she returns to make the offering (such as a garland of jasmine flowers or bananas, of which the spirits are said to be especially fond) promised when the request was made.

The *vihara* (sanctuary) was rebuilt in 1434, 1806, 1894 and, most recently, in 1926. West of the vihara is an enormous stupa containing the ashes of King Ponhea Yat (reigned 1405 to 1467). In a small pavilion on the south side of the passage between the vihara and the stupa is a statue of a smiling and rather plump Madame Penh.

A bit to the north of the vihara and below it is an eclectic shrine dedicated to the genie Preah Chau, who is especially revered by the Vietnamese. On either side of the entrance to the chamber in which a statue of Preah Chau sits are guardian spirits bearing iron bats. On the tile table in front of the two guardian spirits are drawings of Confucius, and two Chinese-style figures of the sages Thang Cheng (on the right) and Thang Thay (on the left). To the left of the central altar is an eight-armed statue of Vishnu.

Down the hill from the shrine is a royal stupa sprouting full-size trees from its roof. For now, the roots are holding the bricks together in their net-like grip, but when the trees die and rot, part of the tower, its bricks pried apart as the roots forced their way between them, will slowly crumble. If you can't make it out to Angkor, this stupa gives a pretty good idea of what the jungle can do (and is doing) to Cambodia's monuments.

At the bottom of the hill on the north-western side is a small zoo, though Wat Phnom's most endearing animal residents, its monkeys, live free in the trees, feasting on people's banana offerings. Elephant rides around the base of Wat Phnom are a favourite attraction on Sundays and holidays; the elephants work regular government business hours (that is, they take a long siesta around

lunch time). Every Thursday at 10 am the weekly national lottery is drawn here.

Wat Ounalom Wat Ounalom, the headquarters of the Cambodian Buddhist patriarchate, is on the south-western corner of the intersection of Lenin Blvd and 154 St (across from Phnom Penh Tourism). Under Pol Pot, the complex, which was founded in 1443 and includes 44 structures, was heavily damaged and its extensive library destroyed. Wat Ounalom was once home to over 500 monks; now there are only 30, including the head of the country's Buddhist hierarchy.

On the 2nd floor of the main building, to the left of the dais, is a statue of Samdech (His Excellency) Huot Tat, Fourth Patriarch of Cambodian Buddhism, who was killed by Pol Pot. The statue, made in 1971 when the patriarch was 80, was thrown in the Mekong but retrieved after 1979.

Nearby, a bookcase holds a few remnants of the once-extensive library of the Buddhist Institute, which was based here until 1975 and is being re-established. To the right of the dais is a statue of a former patriarch of the Thummayuth sect, which is followed by the royal family.

On the 3rd floor of the building is a marble Buddha of Burmese origin broken into pieces by the Khmer Rouge and later reassembled. On the right front corner of the dais on the 3rd floor are the cement remains of a Buddha from which the Khmer Rouge stripped the silver covering. In front of the dais to either side are two glass cases containing flags – each 20 metres long – used during Buddhist celebrations. The walls are decorated with scenes from the life of the Buddha, which were painted when the building was constructed in 1952.

Behind the main building is a stupa containing an eyebrow hair of the Buddha. There is an inscription in Pali over the entrance.

Wat Lang Ka Wat Lang Ka, which is on the southern side of Sivutha Blvd just west of Victory Monument, was almost completely destroyed by Pol Pot. It was the second of Phnom Penh's wats repaired by the post-

1979 government (the first was Wat Ounalom). Around the main building are reconstructed stupas. Both the ground level and 2nd-floor chambers of the vihara have been newly painted with colourful scenes from the life of the Buddha. Fifteen monks live at Wat Lang Ka; 20 years ago there were hundreds.

Wat Koh Wat Koh, on the eastern side of Achar Mean Blvd between 174 St and 178 St, is one of Phnom Penh's oldest pagodas. It was established centuries ago (around the time when Wat Phnom was founded) but only became popular with the masses after the lake surrounding its very small vihara was filled in during the 1950s. Much of the complex, which was damaged by the Khmer Rouge, is now being repaired. There are plans to complete the vihara, construction of which halted in 1975. Today, five monks live at Wat Koh.

To the left of the entrance is a terracotta-coloured obelisk under a wood canopy erected as a memorial to the victims of Pol Pot and soldiers who died fighting his forces. The tower behind the vihara is the stupa of a member of the royal family.

Wat Moha Montrei Wat Moha Montrei, which is one block east of the Olympic Market, is on the southern side of Sivutha Blvd between 163 St and 173 St (across from the National Sports Complex). It was named in honour of one of King Monivong's ministers, Chakrue Ponn, who initiated the founding of the pagoda (*moha montrei* means 'the great minister'). The cement vihara, topped with a 35-metre-high tower, was completed in 1970. Between 1975 and 1979, the building was used to store rice and corn.

Notice the assorted Cambodian touches incorporated in the wall murals of the vihara, which tell the story of the Buddha: the angels accompanying the Buddha to heaven are dressed as classical Khmer dancers, and the assembled officials wear white military uniforms of the Sihanouk period. Along the wall to the left of the dais is a painted and carved

wooden lion from which religious lessons are preached four times a month. The gold-coloured wooden throne nearby is used for the same purpose. All the statues of the Buddha here were made after 1979. Twelve monks live at Wat Moha Montrei, which like many wats, runs an elementary school on the premises.

Nur ul-Ihsan Mosque Nur ul-Ihsan Mosque in Khet Chraing Chamres, founded in 1813, is seven km north of downtown Phnom Penh on National Route 5. According to local people, it was used by the Khmer Rouge as a pigsty and reconsecrated in 1979. It now serves a community of 360 Cham and ethnic-Malay Muslims. A minaret, taller than the nearby coconut palms, was knocked down and has yet to be rebuilt. Next to the mosque is a *madrasa* (religious school). Visitors must remove their shoes before entering the mosque.

To get to Nur ul-Ihsan Mosque, take a bus, Lambretta or remorque-moto from O Russei Market towards Khet Prek Phnou, which is a few km north-west of Khet Chraing Chamres.

An-Nur an-Na'im Mosque The original An-Nur an-Na'im Mosque, once the largest in Phnom Penh, was built in 1901 and razed by the Khmer Rouge. A new, more modest brick structure – topped with a white dome holding a star and crescent aloft – has been under construction by the local Muslim community since 1981. A minaret will be added when funding is found. A madrasa to educate the children of the mosque's 600 families is being built next to the mosque, which is in Chraing Chamres II about one km north of Nur ul-Ihsan Mosque.

Markets
Central Market The dark-yellow Art Deco Central Market, whose central domed hall resembles a Babylonian ziggurat, has four wings filled with shops selling gold and silver jewellery, antique coins, fake name-brand watches and other such items. Around the main building are stalls offering *kramas*,

(checked scarves) stationery, household items, cloth for sarongs, flowers, etc. There are food stalls on the structure's western side, which faces Achar Mean Blvd.

O Russei Market 'Luxury' foodstuffs, costume jewellery and imported toiletries are sold in hundreds of stalls at O Russei Market, which is on 182 St between 111 St and 141 St. The complex also includes scores of food stalls.

Tuol Tom Pong Market Tuol Tom Pong Market, bounded by 155 St on the east, 163 St on the west, 440 St on the north and 450 St on the south, is the city's best source of real and fake antiquities. Items for sale include miniature Buddhas, various ritual objects and old Indochinese coins. There are also quite a few goldsmiths and silversmiths, motorbike parts shops and book vendors; the latter may have maps for sale. There are food stalls in the central section of the market. It is said that Russian expats shop here for vegetables and meat – and that the locals routinely overcharge them.

Olympic Market A great deal of wholesaling is done at the Olympic Market (Marché Olympique), which is near the National Sports Complex and Wat Moha Montrei and is bounded by 193 St, 199 St, 286 St and 283 St. Items for sale include bicycle parts, clothes, electronics and assorted edibles. There are dozens of food stalls in the middle of the market.

Dang Kor Market Dang Kor Market is just north of the intersection of Keo Mony Blvd and Pokambor Blvd, where the modern Municipal Theatre building stands. Not much of interest is sold here, though there are food stalls in the centre of the market area.

The Old Market Household goods, clothes and jewellery are on sale in and around the Old Market (Psar Cha), which is bounded by 13 St, 15 St, 108 St and 110 St. Small restau-rants, food vendors and jewellery stalls are scattered throughout the area.

Other Sights
The following sites of interest are listed from north to south:

Chruoy Changvar Bridge The 700-metre Chruoy Changvar Bridge over the Tonlé Sap River, just off Achar Mean Blvd at 74 St, was once the country's longest; also known as the Tonlé Sap Bridge and the Japanese Bridge, it was blown up in 1975. It was here on the afternoon of 17 April 1975 – the day Phnom Penh fell – that *New York Times* correspondent Sidney Schanberg and four companions were held prisoner by Khmer Rouge fighters and threatened with death; they were saved from summary execution by Dith Pran, whose life under the Khmer Rouge was portrayed in the movie *The Killing Fields*.

These days, the Phnom Penh side of the massive concrete structure has become a hang-out for young couples, especially in the late afternoon and evening. While viewing the river you can enjoy fruit, sugar cane juice and fried foods sold by several refreshment stands. Rumour has it that the Japanese and Indians are looking into repairing the bridge.

Former French Embassy The former French Embassy, which is on the western side of Achar Mean Blvd at 76 St, is now an orphanage whose apparently larcenous residents are blamed by local people for every theft in the neighbourhood. Across the street is the former Korean Embassy.

When Phnom Penh fell on 17 April 1975, about 800 foreigners and 600 Cambodians took refuge in the French Embassy. Within 48 hours, the Khmer Rouge informed the French vice-consul that the new government did not recognise diplomatic privileges and that if all the Cambodians in the compound were not handed over, the lives of the foreigners inside would also be forfeited. Cambodian women married to foreigners could stay, he was told; Cambodian men married to foreign women could not. The foreigners stood and wept as their servants, colleagues, friends, lovers and husbands were escorted out of the embassy gates. At the end of the month, the foreigners were taken out of the country by truck. Almost none of the Cambodians were ever seen again.

Boeng Kak Amusement Park Lakeside Boeng Kak Amusement Park has a small zoo, paddleboats for hire and two restaurants. Its two entrances are 200 metres west of Achar Mean Blvd on 80 St and 86 St.

National Library The National Library (Bibliothèque Nationale; ☎ 2.3249), which is open from 7 to 11.30 am and 2 to 5.30 pm daily except Mondays, is on 92 St next to the Hotel Le Royal. The Khmer Rouge turned the graceful building, constructed in 1924, into a stable and threw many of the books out into the streets, where they were picked up by people who donated them back to the library after 1979.

Today, the National Library has about 100,000 volumes, including many crumbling books in French. Part of the English-language collection consists of books taken from the US Embassy when it was sacked after the communist takeover in 1975. According to Gail Morrison, an Australian volunteer helping to turn the piles of crumbling volumes into a proper library, much of the material is of no value whatsoever, but as a reaction against the Khmer Rouge's contempt for books, the present government forbids the destruction of any printed matter. Cornell University is assisting the National Library to preserve its collection of palm-leaf manuscripts.

Former National Bank The empty lot where the National Bank – blown up by the Khmer Rouge – once stood is on the south-eastern corner of the intersection of Tou Samouth Blvd and 118 St.

English St There is a cluster of private language schools teaching English (and some French) one block west of the National Museum on 184 St between Tou Samouth

Blvd and the back of the Royal Palace compound. Between 5 and 7 pm, the whole area is filled with students who see learning English as the key to making it in post-war Cambodia. This is a good place to meet local young people.

National Sports Complex The National Sports Complex near the intersection of Sivutha Blvd and Achar Hemcheay Blvd includes a sports stadium (which doubles as the site of government-sponsored political rallies) and facilities for swimming, boxing, gymnastics, volleyball and other sports.

Victory Monument Victory Monument, which is at the intersection of Tou Samouth Blvd and Sivutha Blvd, was built in 1958 as an Independence Monument. It is now a memorial to Cambodia's war dead (or at least those the present government considers worthy of remembering). Wreaths are laid here on national holidays. Nearby, beside Lenin Blvd, is the Cambodia-Vietnam Monument.

Prayuvong Buddha Factories In order to replace the countless Buddhas and ritual objects smashed by the Khmer Rouge, a whole little neighbourhood of private workshops producing cement Buddhas, nagas, gingerbread ornamentation and small stupas has grown up on the grounds of Wat Prayuvong. While the graceless cement figures, painted in gaudy colours, are hardly works of art, they are part of an effort by the Cambodian people to restore Buddhism to a place of honour in their reconstituted society.

The Prayuvong Buddha Factories are on the eastern side of Tou Samouth Blvd about 300 metres south of Victory Monument (between 308 St and 310 St). There is a teashop just inside the gate, which is decorated with Bayon-style faces.

Former US Embassy The former US Embassy is on the north-eastern corner of the intersection of Tou Samouth Blvd and Keo Mony Blvd. Much of the US air war in Cambodia (1969 to 1973) was run from here.

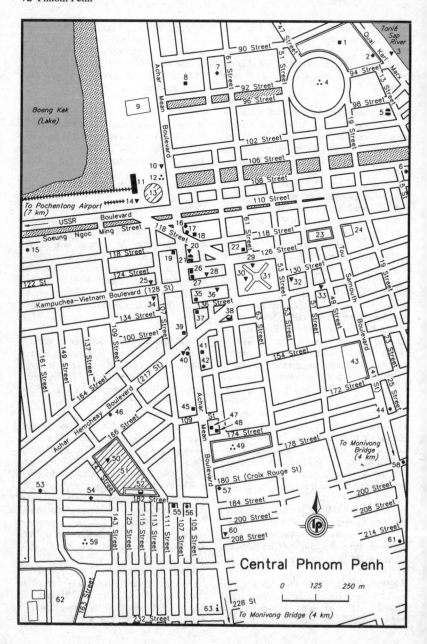

Boeng Kak
(Lake)

Tonlé
Sap
River

To Pochentong Airport
(7 km)

USSR   Boulevard
Soeung Ngoc Ming Street

Achar Mean Boulevard

Kampuchea–Vietnam Boulevard (128 St)

Achar Hemcheay Boulevard (217 St)

Achar Mean Boulevard

To Monivong
Bridge
(4 km)

To Monivong Bridge (4 km)

Central Phnom Penh

0   125   250 m

■ PLACES TO STAY

1	Hotel Wat Phnom
8	Hotel Le Royal
18	Hotel Dosit
19	Hotel Monorom
22	Hotel Apsara
26	Hotel Sukhalay
27	Hotel d'Asie
35	Hotel Santépheap
37	Blue Hotel
39	Hotel Paradis
40	Hotel Pailin
41	Hotel Pacific
45	Hotel Neakpean
47	Hotel Mittapheap
48	Hotel Orchidee
55	Hotel Capitol

▼ PLACES TO EAT

3	Restaurant Tonlé Sap 2
10	Faculty of Medicine Restaurant
14	Holiday Restaurant
20	Restaurant
25	Small Restaurants & Pastry Shops
28	Restaurant Samapheap & the Cafeteria
29	Restaurant Phsathu Thmei
30	Food Stalls
32	Restaurant Sobhamongkol
33	Small Restaurants
34	Restaurant Thmor Da
36	Cafe Champa
40	International Restaurant
50	Food Stalls
60	Soup Restaurant

OTHER

2	Entrance to Hotel Wat Phnom
4	Wat Phnom
5	GPO
6	Old Market
7	National Library
9	Interspoutnik Satellite Ground Station
11	Railway Station
12	Stupa containing Buddha Relic
13	Night Market
15	Council of Ministers
16	Foreign Trade Bank
17	Phnom Penh Airways Office
21	Post/Telephone Office
23	Customs House
24	Former National Bank Site
31	Central Market
38	Psar Thmei Local Bus Terminal
42	Night Market
43	Military Museum (closed)
44	Kampuchean Airlines Booking Office
46	Motorbike Parts Shops
49	Wat Koh
51	O Russei Market
52	O Russei Local Bus Station
53	Motorbike Parts Shop
54	Bicycle Shops
56	Bicycle Shops
57	Ministry of Information & Culture
58	'English Street'
59	Wat Sampao Meas
61	Russian Cultural Centre
62	National Sports Complex
63	General Directorate of Tourism

The building now houses the Department of Fisheries of the Ministry of Agriculture.

On the morning of 12 April 1975, 360 heavily armed US Marines brought in by helicopter secured a landing zone several hundred metres from the embassy. Within hours, 276 people – Americans, Cambodians and others – were evacuated by helicopter relay to US ships in the Gulf of Thailand. Among the last to leave was US Ambassador John Gunther Dean, carrying the embassy's US flag under his arm.

Cham Kar Mon Palace Cham Kar Mon Palace, on the west side of Tou Samouth Blvd between 436 St and 462 St, was once the residence of Prince Sihanouk. The palace, whose name means 'silkworm fields', is now used by visiting heads of state.

Places to Stay

Many of Phnom Penh's hotels are run by assorted organs of the national and municipal governments, which compete with each other for valuable tourist and expat dollars. In 1989 foreign-aid workers, who had until then taken up all but a few of Phnom Penh's hotel rooms, were given the go-ahead to find other quarters, greatly increasing the number of rooms available for tourists.

Subsequently, the room count has grown even more as new, renovated or reopened hotels continue to pop up around town. Despite the increasing number of rooms, space can still be at a premium as the population of aid workers, businesspeople and tourists continues to mushroom. Because of this scarcity, hotel prices in Phnom Penh have escalated rapidly and will probably continue to rise.

Central Market Area Budget travellers arriving in Phnom Penh from Ho Chi Minh City usually head straight for the *Hotel Capitol* on 182 St at the corner of 107 St and just across the road from the O Russei Market and Bus Station. Rooms here with one bed (single or double) cost US$8; with two beds they are US$12. There's a restaurant downstairs which is a convenient meeting place and if there's no room available the English-speaking manager may be able to suggest alternatives.

The four-storey *Hotel Le Royal* (☎ 2.4151, 2.3051) has 82 rooms and is next to the National Library on the corner of Achar Mean Blvd and 92 St (Blvd Pologne). The hotel has certainly gone through several name changes as it was originally the Hotel Le Royal, then became the Hotel Phnom and then the Hotel Samaki (the name means 'solidarity') before recently reverting to Le Royal. Between 1970 and 1975 most journalists working in Phnom Penh stayed here and part of the film *The Killing Fields* was set here (though filmed in Hua Hin in Thailand). When foreign-aid workers set up shop in the country after the Vietnamese takeover, this was again where they stayed. Although there is a swimming pool, the hotel is somewhat neglected but foreign investors are reportedly interested in renovating the hotel, which is now run by the Ministry of Commerce. Rooms in the main building with air-conditioning and refrigerators cost from

US$26 to US$37; three-room bungalows cost US$40 and US$50 a day.

The six-storey *Hotel Monorom* (☎ 2.4549, 2.4951; 68 rooms), run by Phnom Penh Tourism, is on the corner of Achar Mean Blvd and 118 St. This was one of the first hotels to reopen after the Vietnamese takeover. Rooms cost from US$31 to US$50 and there is a great view of the city from the terrace of the 6th-floor restaurant. There is another restaurant on the ground floor fronting 118 St.

The seven-storey *Hotel Sukhalay* (the name means 'good health'; ☎ 2.2403; 60 rooms) at the intersection of Achar Mean St and 126 St belongs to the Cabinet du Conseil des Ministres. There is a wide variety of rooms from US$21 to US$34 or in the annexe at US$15 to US$24. The Sukhalay has a restaurant on the ground floor.

The *Hotel Pailin* (☎ 2.2475; 50 rooms), previously called the White Hotel, is at 219 Achar Mean Blvd, on the south-western corner of the intersection of Achar Mean Blvd and Achar Hemcheay Blvd. Singles here cost US$25, doubles US$48 to US$55. The associated International Restaurant is on the corner. On the north-west corner of the same intersection is the recently opened *Hotel Paradis*, and directly across Achar Mean Blvd from the Pailin is the *Hotel Pacific*.

More new hotels have popped up farther south along Achar Mean Blvd. On the west side of the street at the intersection with 109 St is the *Hotel Neakpoan*. On the opposite side of the road at 262 Achar Mean Blvd, just north of 174 St, is the *Hotel Mittapheap* (☎ 2.3464). Just round the corner on 174 St is the *Hotel Orchidee* (☎ 2.2659) where double rooms cost US$48.

The *Hotel Santépheap* (formerly the Hotel Khemara; the current name means 'peace'; ☎ 2.3227; 43 rooms), which is run by the Commerce Directorate of the Phnom Penh Municipality, is on the corner of Achar Mean Blvd and 136 St (across the street from 169 Achar Mean Blvd). Reception is up one flight of stairs from the entrance, which is on 136 St. There is a restaurant on the ground floor but both hotel and restaurant appear to be closed for renovations.

The *Blue Hotel*, which belongs to the Ministry of National Defence but may become a regular hotel in the near future, is across 136 St from the Hotel Santépheap. The Phnom Penh Municipality's *Hotel d'Asie* (☎ 2.2751, 50 rooms), which is at 136 Achar Mean Blvd on the corner with 128 St (next to the Hotel Sukhalay), is being renovated.

The *Hotel Dosit* was the Hotel of the National People's Bank before it was renovated. It's on 118 St, diagonally opposite the Hotel Monorom and at the back of the Foreign Trade Bank. *Hotel Apsara* (☎ 2.4351) is at 162 61 St, on the corner of 126 St and immediately north of the Central Market.

Along the River Cambodia's biggest and most luxurious hotel, the huge riverside *Hotel Cambodiana* took almost a quarter of a century to complete. Begun around 1967 when Prince Sihanouk was chief of state, the unfinished structure and its spacious grounds were used as a military base by the Lon Nol government. Refugees from the fighting in the countryside sheltered under its concrete roof between 1970 and 1975. Work was resumed in 1987 after a Cambodian expatriate living in Hong Kong and two Singaporeans decided to invest at least US$20 million in the project. It finally opened under the management of the wonderfully named Aggressive Hotel Group but is now part of the Sofitel chain.

The Hotel Cambodiana has restaurants, bars, a swimming pool, health centre, business centre, shops and rooms equipped with everything from central air-conditioning to TV sets with daily video movies. For this unexpected luxury you pay from US$110 to US$170 a day for a double, but, as with so many other hotels in Phnom Penh, prices are likely to rise soon.

In the shadow of the Hotel Cambodiana is the *Cambodiana Inn* (☎ 2.5059; 22 rooms) on Quai Karl Marx near the foot of 240 St. This collection of bungalows is being renovated.

A little north of the Cambodianas is the *Hotel Renakse* (☎ 2.2457) on Lenin Blvd, directly opposite the Silver Pagoda compound of the Royal Palace. This fine old building has 23 rooms, all with attached bathroom and air-conditioning and priced at US$30 to US$35 for doubles. More rooms are planned.

The former French Résidence Supérieure (and later Palais du Gouvernement) is just north-east of Wat Phnom between 90 St and 94 St. Known as the *Hotel Wat Phnom*, it is now an official guest house for high-ranking delegations.

Places to Eat

Food Stalls Food stalls can be found in and around the Central Market (on the western side which faces Kampuchea-Vietnam Blvd), O Russei Market (along 141 St midway between 182 St and 166 St), Tuol Tom Pong Market, the Olympic Market (along 286 St), Dang Kor Market, the Old Market and near the Psar Cha Ministry of Transport Ferry Landing.

In the evening and at night, food stalls pop up between the railway station and USSR Blvd. There is a small night market on the corner of Achar Mean Blvd and 154 St (next to 232 Achar Mean Blvd).

Restaurants – central market area The eatery across the street from the Hotel Monorom (opposite 103 Achar Mean Blvd), signposted in Latin characters simply as Restaurant, is a quiet, well-lit place with good food and decent service. Main dishes start at US$1.

The *Faculty of Medicine Restaurant*, which is on the grounds of the Faculty of Medicine of Phnom Penh University, is adjacent to the square in front of the railway station (on the north-west corner of the intersection of Achar Mean Blvd and 106 St). This open-air place, which serves 'Asian' and French food, is open from 5 am to 9 pm.

The *Restaurant Sereipheap* (the name means 'freedom'; ☎ 2.5837) at 76 Achar Mean Blvd and the *Restaurant Santépheap* (☎ 2.2227), on the corner of Achar Mean

Blvd and 136 St are both closed, presumably for renovation.

The *International Restaurant*, said to be owned by one of Hun Sen's brothers, is a quiet (no band or video!), well-lit place on the ground floor of the Pailin Hotel. The food is decent and reasonably priced and this is a very popular restaurant.

Restaurant Samapheap (the name means 'equality') at 39 128 St (Kampuchea-Vietnam Blvd) is 100 metres west of the Central Market. Main dishes cost from US$1 to US$2.50. Next door at 37 128 St is the *Cafeteria* (open from 6 am to 9 pm), which offers Khmer and European food; the foreign-language menu (in French and Russian) lists only the European fare. Across the street at 26 128 St is the *Soup & Sweets Shop*. The *Dancing Restaurant* (open 6.30 to 11 pm) is a restaurant/nightclub on the 2nd floor of the building across the street from 9 128 St. Take the long flight of stairs on the side of the building nearest the Central Market to get up there from the street. When the government is not enforcing one of its periodic crack-downs on dancing and other forms of entertainment, live bands play here at night.

Continue across Achar Mean Blvd, still on 128 St (Kampuchea-Vietnam Blvd), and the *Restaurant Thmor Da* is just beyond the corner of 107 St. This large, bright, new restaurant is very popular with foreign visitors and aid workers. The Cambodian-style chicken salad is delicious and many other dishes are prepared with real flair. Some can be rather pricey, so check first before ordering anything particularly exotic. There's a separate air-conditioned room. A much smaller establishment with the same name is on the same street but just east of the above restaurant, between Achar Mean Blvd and 107 St.

Restaurant Phsathu Thmei is a proper sit-down restaurant at the northern edge of the Central Market complex (opposite the intersection of 126 St and 61 St). *Restaurant Sobhamongkol*, which has a blue-and-white awning, is east of the Central Market on the south-eastern corner of the intersection of 53 St and 130 St. Two blocks away, on 136 St between 49 St and 51 St, there are several other places to eat. There is a cluster of small restaurants across the street from the western side of the Central Market. There are also a number of small eateries and pastry shops along 128 St between Achar Mean Blvd and 109 St.

There is a popular restaurant renowned among locals for its Vietnamese beef soup (made with white vermicelli) on the north-eastern corner of the intersection of Achar Mean Blvd and 208 St.

Restaurants – Boeng Kak area There are two restaurants in the lakeside Boeng Kak Amusement Park, which is behind the Revolution Hospital (formerly the Calmette Hospital) about 800 metres north of the Hotel Monorom. The park's two entrances are one long block west of Achar Mean Blvd on 80 St and 86 St.

The *Restaurant Raksmey Boeng Kak*, the northernmost of the two, is built out over the lake and can turn out a delicious meal for less than US$5. Try the excellent duck soup or other traditional Cambodian dishes. The other lakeside restaurant is the *Restaurant Thmey Boeng Kak*.

Back on Achar Mean Blvd there's the *Restaurant Chez Lipp* at the corner of 84 St, diagonally opposite the Revolution Hospital. Beside the hospital is the *Restaurant Calmette*.

Restaurants – on the riverfront *Restaurant Tonlé Sap 1* (also known as Restaurant Tespheap Tonlé Sap) is on Quai Karl Marx at the foot of 106 St. The prices are very reasonable. The view of the Tonlé Sap River from the veranda is somewhat spoiled in the evening by swarms of bugs. *Restaurant Tonlé Sap 2* (*Restaurant Ti Pi Tonlé Sap*) is at the intersection of Quai Karl Marx and 94 St (across from the Hotel Wat Phnom). Farther north on the riverside is the *Restaurant Kong Kea*, in the shadow of the collapsed Chruoy Changvar Bridge.

No visit to Phnom Penh is complete without a visit to the *No Problem Café* on

178 St on the north side of the National Museum. Although this is essentially a bar and meeting place, you can get good food and sandwiches at quite reasonable prices. The No Problem is closed on Mondays (see the Entertainment section for more details).

There are quite a few small places to eat along Quai Karl Marx between 154 St and 178 St, near the Royal Palace and Wat Ounalom. The Hotel Cambodiana has a coffee shop, restaurant, bar and other possibilities for anything from a quick snack to the most expensive dining in Phnom Penh.

Entertainment

Bars The Hotel Cambodiana has its *Cyclo Bar* with an evening happy hour and live entertainment, and there are bars in various other larger hotels, but the *No Problem Café* is the number one gathering spot for the city's large expatriate population. This beautifully restored old house on 178 St, on the north side of the National Museum, has a bar, billiard room and a variety of other facilities with a general level of ambience slick enough to fit in anywhere from Sydney to Tokyo or London to LA. To bring you back to reality, there's a clamour of cyclo riders outside the front gate at midnight while behind the building you can find a small iron foundry, an unusual example of Khmer Rouge industrial activity. The No Problem Café is closed on Mondays.

Discos When the government lifted the curfew in the spring of 1989, Phnom Penh developed a lively nightlife that soon came to include some 40 discos. A few weeks later, however, the government suddenly shut everything down; rumour had it that the discos were either a threat to law and order or a potential target of Khmer Rouge terrorism. Many of them have subsequently reappeared and the discos at the *Hotel Le Royal* and the lakeside *Restaurant Thmey Boeng Kak* are particularly popular.

Theatre The Municipal Theatre is a large, modern structure at the intersection of Pokambor Blvd and Keo Mony Blvd.

The Fine Arts School can arrange for performances of classical Cambodian music and dance by its students. For more information, contact either the Fine Arts School (details are listed earlier under Useful Addresses) or the Ministry of Information & Culture (☎ 2.4769) at 395 Achar Mean Blvd.

Things to Buy

Antiques, silver items and jewellery are available from the shops at numbers 163, 139, 105 and 99EO Achar Mean Blvd and on the street that links the Hotel Monorom with the Central Market. There are also a number of jewellery shops specialising in gold and silver in the Central Market, Tuol Tom Pong Market and the Old Market.

The Bijouterie d'État (State Jewellery Shop), run by the National People's Bank, sells items made of gold, silver and precious stones; it is on the north-eastern corner of the intersection of 13 St and 106 St (at 104 St).

The École des Beaux-Arts Shop at the corner of 19 St and 184 St (at the back of the National Museum complex) is open daily except Sunday afternoons from 7 to 11.30 am and from 2 to 5.30 pm. The shop, which belongs to the Fine Arts School, offers wood carvings, papier-mâché masks, stone copies of ancient Khmer art, brass figurines and oil paintings made by the school's students. Profits are divided between the student artists and the school.

Kramas (checked scarves) can be purchased at the Central Market (in the eaves of the main building) and at other marketplaces as well as from the Hotel Monorom gift shop. You can request that unhemmed silk kramas be hemmed on the spot.

Bolts of colourful cloth for sarongs and hols are on sale at Nay Eng, a shop at 108 136 St (opposite the southern side of the Central Market). It is open from 7 am to 9 pm.

There are a number of photo stores selling Kodak and ORWO print film along Achar Mean Blvd, (try numbers 149 and 203 and around the White Hotel) and on 110 St near the Old Market. One-hour colour print processing is available at a store (☎ 2.3137) at

121-123 Achar Mean Blvd (across from the Hotel Sukhalay). Postcards can be surprisingly difficult to find in Phnom Penh – try the bookstalls in the Central Market.

The Diplomatic Store is at 10 Kampuchea-Vietnam Blvd (128 St).

Getting There & Away

Air For information on air service to/from Phnom Penh, see the Getting There & Away and Getting Around chapters.

The Kampuchean Airlines booking office (signposted as the Département de l'Aviation Civil du Cambodge and the Direction of Kampuchea Civil Aviation; ☎ 2.5887) is at 62 Tou Samouth Blvd. Official hours are 7 to 11 am and 2 to 5 pm Monday to Saturday, but in exceptional circumstances it may be possible to purchase tickets during the siesta, after 5 pm and even on Sundays. This office represents Aeroflot, Lao Aviation and Vietnam Airlines, although there is also an Aeroflot office in the Hotel Sukhalay (☎ 2.2403).

Transindo (☎ 2.5629), the agents for Bangkok Airways, flies every day to/from Bangkok. Their office is at 16 Blvd Achar Mean, Quartier Sras Chak, at the northern end of the road, close to the collapsed Chruoy Changvar Bridge. Phnom Penh Airways (☎ 2.6386), which operates to/from Singapore, has its office at the Hotel Dosit at 1 118 St, opposite the Hotel Monorom.

Bus Buses to points north, east and west of Phnom Penh leave from the Olympic Intercity Bus Station (☎ 2.4613), which is on 199 St next to the Olympic Market. Long-haul buses (mostly old Dodge 500s with no aisle and a separate door for each row of seats) depart between 4 and 5 am for Bavet (in Svay Rieng Province near the Moc Bai crossing to Vietnam), Koh Thom (in Kandal Province about 60 km south of Phnom Penh on the west bank of the Bassac River) and the provincial capitals of Battambang (the 290-km trip takes 13 or 14 hours), Kompong Cham, Kompong Chhnang, Kompong Thom, Prey Veng, Pursat and Svay Rieng.

Most buses to destinations south and south-west of Phnom Penh depart from Psar Dang Kor Bus Station, which is on Keo Mony Blvd next to Dang Kor Market (between 336 St and Pokambor Blvd). Daily buses from here serve Chuk, Kampot (a six-hour trip), Kompong Chhnang, Kompong Som (a five-hour trip by express bus), Kompong Trach, Svey Ambov, Takeo and Tuom Luop. Buses leave in the early morning.

At both stations, it is best to purchase tickets at least a day before departure. Intercity bus transport is in a state of flux and departure stations may be changed. Bus travel within Cambodia by foreigners is forbidden at present.

To Ho Chi Minh City Daily buses to Ho Chi Minh City (Saigon) leave at 6 am from an office (☎ 2.3139) on the south-western corner of 211 St and Ok Nga Sou St (182 St). The office, which is across 211 St from number 180 Ok Nga Sou St, is open from 7 to 11 am and from 2 to 7 pm. One-way passage costs less than US$5. The government preference that foreign guests don't avail themselves of the bus services seems to be relaxing when it comes to this particular route.

Train The Phnom Penh Railway Station (☎ 2.3115) is on the western side of Achar Mean Blvd between 106 St and 108 St. Tickets for the Kompong Som line are sold from the caged booths to the right of the station entrance; tickets for the Battambang line are on sale at the windows to the left. The daily train to Kompong Som is scheduled to depart at 6.40 am; the Battambang train is supposed to leave every day at 6 am, arriving at its final stop 12 hours later if there are no glitches.

Tickets can be purchased the day before departure between 3 and 5 pm and on the morning you intend to travel from 5.55 am. Fares are very cheap. The people sleeping all around the station are peasants waiting to return to the provinces after conducting a bit of business in the big city.

For more information on the Cambodian rail system, see the Getting Around chapter.

Service Taxis Service taxis (mostly white Peugeot 404 station wagons) can be hired at Psar Chbam Pao Shared-Taxi Station, which is on National Route 1 near Chbam Pao Market (between 367 St and 369 St). To get there from the city, go south on Tou Samouth Blvd and turn left (eastward) across Monivong Bridge.

In the mornings, there are regular runs from here to Neak Luong (the Mekong ferry crossing on National Route 1), Svey Rieng and Bavet, which is near the Moc Bai crossing into Vietnam. Transport to Koki Picnic Area is also available. If you have all the necessary permits, it may be possible to rent a taxi here; the cost, depending on the distance, starts at about US$25 a day.

River Transport Large government-run ferries to Kompong Cham, Kratie, Stung Treng, Kompong Chhnang and Phnom Krom (11 km south of Siem Reap) depart from the Psar Cha Ministry of Transport Ferry Landing (☎ 2.5619), which is on Quai Karl Marx between 102 St and 104 St.

There is a service to Kompong Cham and Kratie once every three days. The ferry sets sail from Phnom Penh at 8.30 am, overnighting at Prek Por (whence it departs at 4.30 am on the second day) and docking at Kompong Cham around 8 am. The vessel spends a second night at Chlong (whence it departs at 5 am on the third day of the trip) before finally pulling into Kratie at about 7 am. The ferries to Stung Treng operate only from September to January; during the rest of the year, the level of the river is too low. The run from Kratie to Stung Treng takes 10 to 12 hours. Ferries to Siem Reap depart at 8 am and arrive in Kompong Chhnang at 4 pm or so, continuing across the Tonlé Sap the next morning.

Passenger ferries to Kompong Cham and ports along the way (including Pras Prasap, Roca Kong, Prek Por and Oleng) depart from the Psar Cha Municipal Ferry Landing, which is on Quai Karl Marx between 106 St

and 108 St (next to Restaurant Tonlé Sap 1). The ferry begins its daily upriver journey at 7 am, arriving in Kompong Cham at 5 or 6 pm; the return trip is faster. Passage from Phnom Penh to Kompong Cham costs about US$1.

Passenger and goods ferries to Vietnam leave from the Chbam Pao Ferry Landing. A ferry departs daily at 3 pm, arriving five or six hours later at the Mekong River border landing of Kom Samnor, where passengers transfer (either immediately or the next morning) to Vietnamese ferries for passage to Phu Chau (Tan Chau) and beyond. The usually overloaded ferries, which lack even rudimentary safety equipment, are simple wooden affairs offering only deck-class passage, which costs US$2. To get to Chbam Pao Ferry Landing, go a few hundred metres south from Chbam Pao Market on 369 St and turn right down an unmarked alleyway opposite number 210 369 St.

Getting Around
To/From the Airport Pochentong International Airport is seven km west of the centre of Phnom Penh out USSR Blvd or Kampuchea-Vietnam Blvd. Locals may

need special authorisation to enter the airport complex. Passenger vehicles departing from O Russei Market to Pochentong pass by the gate to the airport terminal.

Bus Buses and small passenger trucks serving Phnom Penh's suburbs depart from a parking lot on 182 St next to O Russei Market; the station operates from about 5.30 am until sundown. Vehicles from here go to Chbam Pao (on National Route 1 across Monivong Bridge from the city), Champu Vonn, Chraing Chamres (north of the city along National Route 5), Kanthoutt, Pochentong and Pochentong Airport (west of the city on National Route 3) and Takmau (south of the city on National Route 2).

The Psar Thmei Local Bus Terminal is 100 metres south-west of the Central Market at the intersection of Achar Hemcheay Blvd and 136 St. Buses to Takmau run twice an hour between 5.30 am and 5.30 pm. There is twice-hourly service (on the hour and half-hour) to Chbam Pao, Chraing Chamres and Takmau from about 5.30 am to 5 pm.

Buses from the lot in front of Chbam Pao Market (across Monivong Bridge from the city) go to O Russei Market and the Central Market.

Bicycle There are two clusters of bicycle shops near O Russei Market: one is on 182 St across the street from number 23 (between Achar Mean Blvd and O Russei Market) and the other is on 182 St between 141 St and 163 St (between O Russei Market and Achar Hemcheay Blvd). Bicycle parts are also sold at the Olympic Market.

Bicycles for sale in Phnom Penh include cheap Vietnamese bicycles starting at US$20, small thick-framed Soviet-made bicycles for US$24 and up and deluxe Thai models for around US$80.

Cyclo Cyclos or samlors, which can be found cruising around town and at marketplaces, are a great way to see the city. Some of the drivers who hang out near major hotels speak a bit of English or French. They probably work for the secret police, but then again so does everyone else you are likely to come in contact with. A one-km ride around the city centre should cost about US$0.50. Expats adept at bargaining report hiring samlor at a rate of about US$0.35 an hour but the average visitor will probably have to pay closer to US$1.

Motorbikes There are motorbike parts stores on Achar Hemcheay Blvd, between 109 St and 139 St, and on 182 St near the intersection with Achar Hemcheay Blvd (217 St).

Driving Petrol stations are open from 7 to 10 am and from 2 to 3.30 pm daily except Sundays. When the petrol stations are closed, black market petrol, sold in one-litre glass bottles, can be purchased from kerbside vendors, who are especially numerous near the Central Market and other marketplaces.

River Transport Ferries across the Tonlé Sap River dock at the Psar Cha Ministry of Transport Ferry Landing.

A motorised boat large enough for 10 people can be chartered from Phnom Penh Tourism for US$10 an hour.

Top: Preah Neak Pean (TW)
Left: Preah Khan (TW)
Right: Preah Khan guard (TW)

Top Left: Ta Prohm, Angkor (TW)
Top Right: Ta Prohm, Angkor (TW)
Bottom Left: Angkor Thom, South Gate (TW)
Bottom Right: Rre Rup Temple (TW)

Top: Kids at Preah Ko (TW)
Left: Phnom Penh kids (TW)
Right: Royal Palace guard (TW)

Top: Preah Ko, Roluos Group (TW)
Left: Bakong, Roluos Group (TW)
Right: Lolei, Roluos Group (TW)

Around Phnom Penh

North of Phnom Penh

PREK KDAM FERRY

The Prek Kdam Ferry, 32 km north of central Phnom Penh, crosses the Tonlé Sap River to connect National Route 5 with National Route 6, which goes to Kompong Thom, Siem Reap and, via National Route 7, to Kompong Cham. There are lots of refreshment stands near the landings.

UDONG ឧដុង្គ

Udong ('the Victorious') served as the capital of Cambodia under several sovereigns between 1618 and 1866. A number of them, including King Norodom, were crowned here. Phnom Udong, a beautiful site for a picnic, is a bit south of the old capital. It consists of two parallel ridges, both of which offer great views of the Cambodian countryside and its innumerable sugar palm trees. From Phnom Penh's taller buildings (including the Hotel Monorom), the bluffs of Udong appear as two symmetrical hills – one of which is topped with spires – in the middle the plains stretching northward from the city.

One monk lives in a tiny (two by 2½-metre) thatch house built on the low ridge linking the two hills. Nearby is a simple thatch vihara (sanctuary).

The smaller ridge, which is oriented north-west to south-east, has two structures – both heavily damaged – and several stupas on top. Ta San Mosque, which is to the right from the top of the path up from the monk's house, faces westward towards Mecca. Only the bullet and shrapnel-pocked walls survived the years of Khmer Rouge rule. The Cham Muslims plan to rebuild it and have already erected a temporary thatch structure nearby. From the mosque you can see, across the plains to the south, Phnom Vihear Leu, a small hill on which a vihara stands between two white poles. To the right of the vihara is

a building used as a prison under Pol Pot. To the left of the vihara and below it is a pagoda known as Arey Ka Sap.

North-west of the mosque (to the left from the top of the path) are the ruins of Vihear Preah Chaul Nipean, a laterite vihara once home to a large reclining Buddha that was blown to bits by Pol Pot's forces. All around lie the headless bodies and shattered faces of Buddhas smashed during the Khmer Rouge's orgy of destruction.

The larger, uneven ridge, Phnom Preah Reach Throap ('Hill of the Royal Fortune'), is so named because a 16th century Khmer king is said to have hidden the national treasury here during a war with the Thais. The most impressive structure on Phnom Preah Reach Throap (which is also known as Phnom Ath Roes and Phnom Preah Chet Roes) is Vihear Preah Ath Roes, 'Vihara of the 18-Cubit (nine-metre) Buddha'. The vihara and the Buddha, dedicated in 1911 by King Sisowath, were blown up by the Khmer Rouge in 1977; only sections of the metre-thick walls, the bases of eight enormous columns and the right arm and part of the right side of the Buddha remain.

About 120 metres north-west of Vihear Preah Ath Roes is a line of small viharas. The first is Vihear Preah Ko, a brick-roofed structure inside of which is a statue of Preah Ko, the sacred bull; the original of this statue was carried away by the Thais long ago. The second structure, which has a seated Buddha inside, is Vihear Preah Keo. The third is Vihear Prak Neak, its cracked laterite walls topped with a temporary thatch roof. Inside is a seated Buddha guarded by a naga (*prak neak* means 'protected by a naga').

At the north-west extremity of the ridge stand three large stupas. The first one you come to is the cement Chet Dey Mak Proum, the final resting place of King Monivong (ruled 1927 to 1941). Decorated with Garudas, floral designs and elephants, it has four Bayon-style faces on top. The middle stupa, Tray Troeng, is decorated with coloured tiles; it was built in 1891 by King Norodom for the ashes of his father, King Ang Duong (ruled 1845 to 1859). According to another version of events, King Ang Duong was buried next to the Silver Pagoda in Phnom Penh. The third stupa, Damrei Sam Poan, was erected by King Chey Chethar II (ruled 1618 to 1626) for the ashes of his predecessor, King Soriyopor (ruled 1601 to 1618).

An eastward-oriented laterite staircase leads down the hillside from the stupa of King Monivong. Just north of its base is a pavilion decorated with graphic murals depicting Khmer Rouge atrocities. Across the road, 300 metres due west of the three stupas (on the other side of the ridge), is a memorial to the victims of Pol Pot containing the bones of some of the people who were buried in approximately 100 mass graves, each containing about a dozen bodies.

Instruments of torture were unearthed along with the bones when a number of the two by 2½-metre pits were disinterred in 1981 and 1982.

Getting There & Away
Udong is 40 km from the capital. To get there, head north out of Phnom Penh on National Route 5. Continue on past Prek Kdam Ferry for 4½ km and turn left (southward) at the roadblock and bunker. Udong is 3½ km south of the turnoff; the access road goes through the village of Psar Dek Krom and passes by a memorial to Pol Pot's victims and a structure known as the Blue Stupa before arriving at a short staircase. Stick to the paths – there may be mines around here.

To travel to Udong from Phnom Penh by bus, take any vehicle heading for Kompong Chhnang or Battambang; get off at the roadblock and bunker.

South of Phnom Penh

There are several historical sites of interest in Takeo Province. Most of them can be visited on day trips from Phnom Penh.

TONLÉ BATI ទន្លេបាទី
Ta Prohm Temple
The laterite Temple of Ta Prohm was built by King Jayavarman VII (ruled 1181 to 1201) on the site of a 6th century Khmer shrine. A stele found here dates from 1574. The site is open all day every day. A Khmer-speaking guide can be hired for US$0.30 to US$0.60, though on Sundays the guides are usually overwhelmed with business.

The main sanctuary consists of five chambers; in each is a statue or linga (or what is left of a statue after the destruction wrought by the Khmer Rouge).

A few metres to the right of the main (eastward-facing) entrance to the sanctuary building, about three metres above the ground, is a bas-relief carving of a woman carrying an object on her head and a man bowing to another, larger woman. The smaller woman, who has just given birth, did not show proper respect for the midwife (the larger woman). As a result, she has been condemned to carry the afterbirth around on her head in a box for the rest of her life. The prostrate man, the smaller woman's husband, is begging that the midwife grant his wife forgiveness.

Around the corner to the right from the northern entrance of the sanctuary building, about 3½ metres above the ground, is a bas-relief scene in which a king, about 20 cm high, sits to the right of his wife, who is slightly smaller. Because she has been unfaithful, a servant is shown in the scene below putting her to death by trampling her with a horse.

Inside the north gate is a badly damaged statue of the Hindu god Preah Noreay. Women come here to pray that they be granted a child.

Yeay Peau Temple
Yeay Peau Temple, named for its builder, King Ta Prohm's mother Yeay (Madame) Peau, is a small structure 150 metres north of Ta Prohm Temple. Inside, there is a statue of Yeay Peau standing next to a seated Buddha.

Nearby is Wat Tonlé Bati, a modern cement structure heavily damaged by the

Ta Prohm, Tonlé Bati

Khmer Rouge. The only remnant of the pagoda's pre-1975 complement of statues is an 80-cm-high Buddha's head made of metal.

The legend of Yeay Peau Temple goes as follows:

During the time of the building of Angkor Wat (the early 12th century), King Preah Ket Mealea, while on a trip away from Angkor, passed through Tonlé Bati, where he spied Peau, the beautiful daughter of a rich fish merchant. The king fell in love with Peau, who was famous for her long hair (which was always perfumed) and they slept together. Peau fell pregnant but after three months the king had to return to Angkor Wat. When he left he gave her his royal seal ring and a sacred dagger and requested that if the child were a boy, he should be sent to join his father at Angkor when he grew older; but if the child were a girl, she was to remain with her mother.

The child was a boy and Peau named him Prohm. As he grew up, Prohm exhibited great physical strength and an aggressive temperament. When the other children teased him for not having a father, Prohm would return home and ask of his mother, 'Who is my father?', but she refused to tell him.

When Prohm was old enough Peau finally informed him of his parentage. He took the royal seal ring and the sacred dagger and set out for Angkor Wat to find his father. The king, recognising the ring and the dagger, invited him to live with him at Angkor.

After a number of years had passed, Prohm requested his father's permission to visit Tonlé Bati. This was granted, and he set out on the long journey. When he arrived in Tonlé Bati, Prohm did not recognise his mother, who had not aged at all during the time he had been away. Taken by her beauty, he asked her to become his wife. Peau rejected his offer, explaining that she was his mother, but he refused to believe her and continued to insist that she marry him.

To settle the matter, Peau suggested that both she and Prohm construct a temple; whoever finished first would get his or her way in the matter. Prohm agreed, sure that he could easily win the contest. But Peau had a plan. On her suggestion, the contest was to last from sundown until the appearance of the morning star. Two teams formed: all the men of the area joined together to help Prohm while all the women came to assist Peau. In the middle of the night, after work had been going on for many hours, Peau sent aloft an artificial morning star lit with candles. The men, thinking it was morning and certain that the women could not possibly have finished their temple, went to sleep; but the women kept on working and completed Peau's temple by morn. When the men awoke and realised that they had been defeated, Prohm prostrated himself before Peau and recognised her as his mother.

The Lakefront

About 300 metres north-west of Ta Prohm Temple, a long, narrow peninsula juts into the Bati River. On Sundays, it is packed with picnickers and vendors selling food, drink and fruit. During the rest of the week, however, few people come here and there are no food stands around.

Getting There & Away

The access road to Ta Prohm Temple, which is in the Tonlé Bati district of Takeo Province, intersects National Route 2 at a point 33 km south of downtown Phnom Penh, 21 km north of the access road to Phnom Chisor and 44 km north of Takeo. The temple is 2.5 km from the highway. Any bus linking Phnom Penh with the town of Takeo by way of National Route 2 will pass by the access road.

PHNOM CHISOR

The main temple on the top of Phnom Chisor stands at the eastern side of the hilltop in a flat area measuring about 80 by 100 metres. Constructed of laterite and brick with carved lintels of sandstone, the complex is surrounded by the partially ruined walls of a 2½-metre-wide gallery with inward-facing windows.

Inscriptions found here date from the 11th century, when this site was known as Suryagiri. The wooden doors to the sanctuary in the centre of the complex, which open to the east, are decorated with carvings of figures standing on pigs. Inside the sanctuary there are statues of the Buddha.

On the plain to the east of Phnom Chisor are two other Khmer temples, Sen Thmol (at the bottom of Phnom Chisor) and Sen Ravang (farther east), and the former sacred pond of Tonlé Om; all three form a straight line with Phnom Chisor. During rituals held here 900 years ago, the Brahmins and their entourage would climb up to Suryagiri from

this direction on a monumental stairway of 400 steps.

There is a spectacular view of the temples and the surrounding plains from the roofless gallery opposite the wooden doors to the central shrine.

Near the main temple are a modern Buddhist vihara and structures used by the monks who live here. Most of these buildings were damaged during the Pol Pot period.

At the base of Phnom Chisor near the trailhead of the northern path is a quarry where peasants eke out a living prying large boulders out of the hillside and cracking them apart with hammers to make gravel. Each month, a family with all its members working can produce about 20 cubic metres of gravel, which is used for paving roads and in construction. Each cubic metre sells for the equivalent of about US$1.

Getting There & Away

The intersection of National Route 2 with the eastward-bound access road to Phnom Chisor is marked by the two brick towers of Prasat Neang Khmau (the Temple of the Black Virgin), which may have once served as a sanctuary to Kali, the dark goddess of destruction.

Prasat Neang Khmau is on National Route 2 at a point 55 km south of central Phnom Penh, 21 km south of the turnoff to Tonlé Bati and 23 km north of Takeo. The distance from the highway to the base of the hill is a bit over four km.

There are two paths up the 100-metre-high ridge, which takes about 15 minutes to climb. The northern path, which has a mild gradient, begins at a cement pavilion whose windows are shaped like the squared-off silhouette of a bell and which is topped with a miniature replica of an Angkor-style tower. The steeper southern route, which begins 600 metres south of the northern path, consists of a long stairway. A good way to see the view in all directions is to go up the northern path and to come down the southern stairway.

TAKEO តាកែវ

Takeo, capital of a province of the same name, is an extremely quiet little town. There is nothing to do in Takeo, although the town can be used as a base to explore the countryside and nearby historical sites such as Tonlé Bati, Phnom Chisor and Phnom Da (Angkor Borei).

Information

Although there are plans to set up a provincial tourism authority, until this is done the only local source of information on the area will continue to be the provincial people's committee, which has its headquarters in Takeo.

Street names and numbers are not used in Takeo. The northern edge of town abuts Takeo Lake.

Post The post office, which has a phone link to Phnom Penh, is in the western part of town.

Places to Stay

The government guest house, the three-storey *Hotel Takeo* (☎ 6 via the Takeo exchange; 16 beds), is 400 metres north of town on a promontory that juts into Takeo Lake. The Khmer Rouge destroyed a Buddhist pagoda that once stood on this site, constructing the present structure for the use of Chinese experts.

Places to Eat

Restaurant Stung Takeo, which overlooks the Takeo River, is on the road that demarcates the eastern extremity of town. *Restaurant Youvchun* in Takeo's eastern section and *Restaurant Phnom Da* in the southern part of town are not far away.

Getting There & Away

National Route 3, which links Phnom Penh with Kompong Som, is in much better condition than National Route 2, the parallel route that passes through Takmau and goes via Tonlé Bati and Phnom Chisor. Takeo is 83 km from Phnom Penh by National Route

3 and 77 km from the capital by National Route 2.

The Takeo Bus Station is in the southern part of town next to the market. Trains running between Phnom Penh and Kompong Som stop at a railway station a few km north of town.

ANGKOR BOREI អង្គរបុរី
& PHNOM DA ភ្នំដា

Angkor Borei was known as Vyadhapura when it served as the capital of Water Chenla in the 8th century. Four artificial caves, built as shrines, are carved into the north-east wall of Phnom Da, a hill south of Vyadhapura. On top of Phnom Da is a square laterite tower open to the north.

Angkor Borei and Phnom Da are about 20 km east of Takeo along Canal Number 15.

West of Phnom Penh

KOKI BEACH កោះគគីរ

The weekly stampede to Koki Beach is a peculiarly Cambodian institution, a mixture of the universal love of picnicking by the water with the unique Khmer fondness for lounging about on mats at midday in structures built on stilts. It works like this: for US$0.30 or so an hour, families or groups of picnickers rent an area about 2½ metres square on a long raised pier made of split bamboo covered with reed mats. Overhead is a thatch roof to shelter everyone from the midday sun. On Sundays, these piers are jam-packed with Phnom Penhois: wealthy families who drove out in the family car, students who came by bicycle, and less well-off families who all piled onto a remorque-moto. They have come to eat, talk, swim and nap. Be sure to agree on the price *before* you rent a space.

Places to Eat

On Sundays, all sorts of food (grilled chicken and fish, rice, fruit, etc) are sold at Koki Beach, though at prices higher than in Phnom Penh. The beach is almost deserted during the rest of the week, but food is available at restaurants along National Route 1 between the Koki turnoff and the capital.

Getting There & Away

Koki Beach is in Kandal Province in the Koki sub-district of Kien Svay district. To get there from the capital, turn left off National Route 1 (which links Phnom Penh with Saigon) at a point 12 km east of Monivong Bridge. There are service taxis to Koki from the Chbam Pao Shared-Taxi Station, which is just east of Monivong Bridge.

Angkor

The famous temples of Angkor, built between seven and 11 centuries ago when Khmer civilisation was at the height of its extraordinary creativity, constitute one of humankind's most magnificent architectural achievements. From Angkor, the kings of the mighty Khmer Empire ruled over a vast territory that extended from the tip of what is now southern Vietnam northward to Yunnan in China and from Vietnam westward to the Bay of Bengal. Angkor's 100 or so temples constitute the sacred skeleton of a spectacular administrative and religious centre whose houses, public buildings and palaces were constructed of wood – now long decayed – because the right to dwell in structures of brick or stone was reserved for the gods.

SIEM REAP

The town of Siem Reap, whose population is rebounding towards the pre-war total of 10,000, is only a few km from the temples of Angkor and serves as a base for visits to the monuments. The name Siem Reap (pronounced see-EM ree-EP) means 'Siamese Defeated' (*Siem* means 'Siamese' (Thais); *Reap* means 'defeated'). Commodities produced in the area of Siem Reap include freshwater fish, wood and rice.

Information

Tourist Office The desk of Angkor Tourism, the government tourism authority in the Angkor area, is in the Grand Hotel d'Angkor, although it may move from there when the hotel is redeveloped. Angkor Tourism's principal activity is handling visitors booked on tours but they can advise on guest house accommodation. See Information in the following Temples of Angkor section for details about the Angkor visitors' fee.

Angkor Conservation Angkor Conservation (or Angkor Conservancy; in French Conservation d'Angkor; ☎ 82), which has official responsibility for the study, preservation and upkeep of the Angkor monuments, has its headquarters in a large compound between Siem Reap and Angkor Wat. Once home to the great French archaeologist George Groslier, it is now used as a base of operations by Angkor Conservation's two English-speaking guides, 100 other employees (there were once 1000) and the Indian and Polish teams that have been working on Angkor Wat and the Bayon.

Over 5000 statues, lingas and inscribed steles found in the vicinity of Angkor are stored by Angkor Conservation at its headquarters, because of the impossibility of preventing thefts from the hundreds of sites where these artefacts were found. As a result, the finest statuary you will see at Angkor is inside Angkor Conservation's warehouses, meticulously numbered and catalogued but in no way arranged for convenient public viewing. In fact, special permission from provincial authorities is required even to visit the compound; for details, enquire at the front desk of the Grand Hotel d'Angkor.

To get to Angkor Conservation's headquarters, go northward from the Grand Hotel d'Angkor for 1.3 km and take a hard right, continuing south-eastward for 300 metres until you come to an enclosure whose perimeter wall has metal spikes sticking out of the top.

Post & Telecommunications The post office is along the river 400 metres south of the Grand Hotel d'Angkor. It is open daily from 7 to 11.30 am and from 2 to 5 pm. When the lines aren't down, phone calls can theoretically be made to Phnom Penh from here between 8 and 11 am, from 3 to 5 pm and possibly from 7 to 8 pm as well. Telegraph service is also available – usually.

It is possible to telephone to Phnom Penh from the Grand Hotel d'Angkor between 7 and 11 am and from 1 to 5 pm. Letters can be mailed at the reception desk.

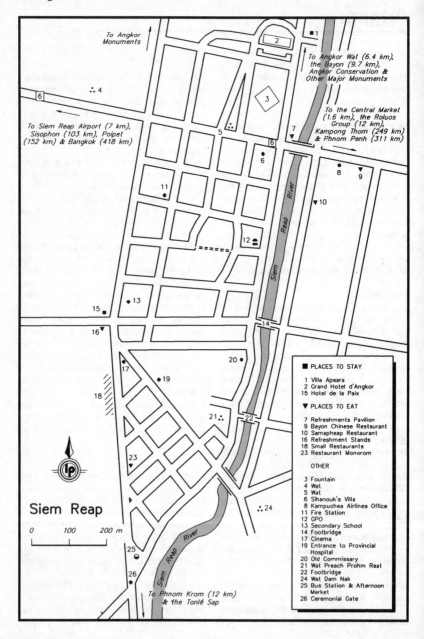

To Angkor
Monuments

To Angkor Wat (6.4 km),
the Bayon (9.7 km),
Angkor Conservation &
Other Major Monuments

To the Central Market
(1.6 km), the Roluos
Group (12 km),
Kampong Thom (249 km)
& Phnom Penh (311 km)

To Siem Reap Airport (7 km),
Sisophon (103 km), Poipet
(152 km) & Bangkok (418 km)

Reap River

Siem

■ PLACES TO STAY

1 Villa Apsara
2 Grand Hotel d'Angkor
15 Hotel de la Paix

▼ PLACES TO EAT

7 Refreshments Pavilion
9 Bayon Chinese Restaurant
10 Samapheap Restaurant
16 Refreshment Stands
18 Small Restaurants
23 Restaurant Monorom

OTHER

3 Fountain
4 Wat
5 Wat
8 Sihanouk's Villa
8 Kampuchea Airlines Office
11 Fire Station
12 GPO
13 Secondary School
14 Footbridge
17 Cinema
19 Entrance to Provincial
   Hospital
20 Old Commissary
21 Wat Preach Prohm Reat
22 Footbridge
24 Wat Dam Nak
25 Bus Station & Afternoon
   Market
26 Ceremonial Gate

Siem Reap

0   100   200 m

Siem Reap River

To Phnom Krom (12 km)
& the Tonlé Sap

Security Some areas in and around the temple complexes have been mined! Visitors should *not* stray from clearly marked paths. Until the war ends, keep in touch with local military authorities to make sure that the trails where you're going have not been booby-trapped to blow up infiltrators. Visitors should be cautious when visiting remote sites if they are alone: unfortunately, the soldiers stationed in the vicinity of Angkor have been known to rob tourists. In the past couple of years the list of sites which you may visit has grown considerably and you are now free to visit most of them without a guide or escort.

Town Centre

The town centre of Siem Reap was blocked off after the arrival of Vietnamese troops in 1979. Almost all of the security barricades have now been removed and the once derelict buildings are gradually being restored and reoccupied. In the late afternoon a colourful little night market operates at the southern corner of the town centre.

Central Market

Siem Reap's new, covered Central Market is 1.6 km east of the Siem Reap River (towards Roluos) on the south side of National Route 6.

Places to Stay

As in Phnom Penh, there is a great deal of hotel construction and renovation activity underway. Prices have been rising rapidly and will continue to rise, but cheaper guest houses are also starting to open. At first these guest houses did not have any signs but they can be found along the road parallel to the river and one block to the east. Enquire there, in the restaurants or at Angkor Tourism. Prices are typically around US$10 to US$15.

The venerable old *Grand Hotel d'Angkor* (☎ 15) was built in 1928 and has 62 rooms, half of them equipped with air-conditioning. A private hotel management group took over operation of the hotel in 1992 and immediately started making repairs to the decrepit wiring and plumbing. As this work is carried out, the room prices of US$25/32 including breakfast are likely to rise, but the longer term intention is to renovate the hotel totally and restore it to its former grandeur. When this operation is completed, the prices will be increased dramatically. Meanwhile, the rooms are spacious if a little threadbare and have attached bathrooms.

Right across the road from the Grand Hotel d'Angkor is the recently reopened *Villa Apsara* which has rooms at US$32/40 with attached bathroom. The plumbing and other facilities work reasonably well here although towel rails and other equipment are still prone to falling off the walls. The Villa Apsara even has a swimming pool though they haven't worked out how to fill it yet.

The three-storey *Hotel de la Paix* (☎ 41) was due to reopen by mid-1992, having been completely renovated from top to bottom. Several other new hotels are also said to be underway in Siem Reap.

The former *Auberge Royale*, once the finest hotel in the area, was razed by the Khmer Rouge. Only the skeleton of the old *Air France Hotel* is still standing.

Places to Eat

The restaurant picture in Siem Reap is also changing fast. At the Grand Hotel d'Angkor foreigners pay US$6 for lunch or dinner, US$3 for breakfast. For guests at the hotel breakfast is included in the tariff. The food is edible but uninspired but standards will undoubtedly rise as the hotel is renovated.

There are a number of other places to eat around town, including the *Bayon Chinese Restaurant* on National Route 6, about 200 metres east of the Siem Reap River. Beside the river, just south of Route 6, is the *Samapheap Restaurant* with excellent Cambodian food. You can eat very well here for US$2 to US$3 and at night it's crowded with aid workers and UN employees.

In the town centre area the *Restaurant Monorom* is another new addition and serves good Chinese food at similar prices to the Samapheap. There are several refreshment stands near the Hotel de la Paix and an open-air refreshments pavilion beside the river, south of the Grand Hotel d'Angkor.

There is a stand opposite the main entrance to Angkor Wat and children scuttle around the main temple sites selling cold soft drinks.

Entertainment

The cinema 120 metres south of the Hotel de la Paix screens video-cassettes. There's another one on Route 6, across from the Bayon Chinese Restaurant.

Things to Buy

There is a photo shop on National Route 6, a few hundred metres east of the bridge over the Siem Reap River. They sell B&W photo prints for 100 riels which can be used as postcards. The Grand Hotel d'Angkor has a small gift shop.

At a number of temple sites there are local souvenir sellers with temple bas-relief rubbings, curious musical instruments, crossbows, ornamental knives and other local crafts.

Getting There & Away

Air At present, the only official way into or out of Siem Reap is by air from Phnom Penh. There are rumours of direct Bangkok-Siem Reap flights commencing soon. Air Kampuchea usually has two flights a day between Phnom Penh and Siem Reap. The round-trip costs US$91 (US$43 each way plus US$5 for airport taxes) and the 40-minute flight is usually operated by turboprop Antonov An-24s, although jet Tupolev Tu-134s may also be used.

Siem Reap Airport is seven km north-west of town and four km due west of Angkor Wat. All flights are met by a bus belonging to Angkor Tourism – this service is part of what your US$120 visitors' fee pays for. For some reason, when you arrive, officials of Angkor Tourism collect your return air tickets. Be sure to make reservations out of Siem Reap as soon as you land.

The Kampuchean Airlines office, now closed, is in a building on the south side of National Route 6, about 100 metres east of the bridge over the Siem Reap River. Until this office reopens, all business with Kampuchean Airlines must be conducted through their representatives at the airport; for more information, ask at the front desk of the Grand Hotel d'Angkor.

Overland Land distances from Siem Reap are:

Phnom Penh	311 km (National Route 6)
Battambang	183 km
Kompong Thom	249 km
Poipet (Thai border)	152 km
Sisophon	103 km

National Route 6 and the road between Siem Reap and Battambang via Sisophon are in an advanced state of dilapidation, in part because of repeated rebel attacks. Nevertheless, the Thais are working on clearing the road around the border area and vehicles are, supposedly, starting to come through from Thailand. The drive from Phnom Penh to Siem Reap takes two days and although foreigners are not, officially, allowed to travel along this route an occasional visitor does manage to sneak through. At present, both roads pass through contested territory.

By land, Angkor is 418 km from Bangkok via the border crossing between Poipet, Cambodia and Aranyaprathet, Thailand. The road between Siem Reap and the frontier is in great need of repair.

Ferry Ferries from Phnom Penh to Phnom Krom, 11 km south of Siem Reap, depart from the capital's Psar Cha Ministry of Transport Ferry Landing, which is on Quai Karl Marx between 102 St and 104 St. The trip takes two days, with an overnight stay at Kompong Chhnang, but, again, foreign visitors are not supposed to travel by this means.

Getting Around

Bicycle & Motorbike The Grand Hotel d'Angkor rents bicycles at a very steep US$2 an hour but already bicycle rental from other sources is becoming possible. Visitors staying at Siem Reap guest houses have also been able to rent motorcycles.

Car & Minibus Angkor Tourism take their tour visitors around the ruins in cars or minibuses which can be rented from around US$40 a day with a driver.

Cyclo You can get around Siem Reap itself in the town's unique and rather uncomfortable cyclos which are essentially standard bicycles with a two-seat trailer in hitch. You can reach anywhere in town for less than 500 riel.

THE TEMPLES OF ANGKOR

Between the 9th and the 13th centuries, a succession of Khmer kings who ruled from Angkor utilised the vast wealth and huge labour force of their empire to carry out a series of monumental construction projects intended to glorify both themselves and their capitals, a succession of which were built in the vicinity of Siem Reap. Over the course of this period, Khmer architecture developed and evolved, in part reflecting the change in religious focus from the Hindu cult of the god Shiva to that of Vishnu and then to a form of Mahayana Buddhism centred on Avalokitesvara.

The monuments of Angkor (the name is a corruption of *Nagara*, 'the City') were designed on the basis of political and religious conceptions of Indian origin that were modified by the Khmers to suit local conditions. The successive cities at Angkor were centred on a temple mountain identified with Mt Meru, home of the gods in Hindu cosmology, which served as both the centre of the earthly kingdom over which the king ruled and the symbolic centre of the universe within which the kingdom existed. The temple mountain functioned as the locus of the cult of the devaraja (god-king), through which the king's sacred personality – the very essence of the kingdom – was enshrined in a linga and worshipped. Upon his death, the temple became the god-king's mausoleum.

The first such central temple mountain,

built during the rule of Yasovarman I (reigned 889 to 910), was grafted onto the only natural hill in the area, Phnom Bakheng. Later, Mt Meru was represented by a series of pyramid temples, including Phimeanakas, erected by Jayavarman V (reigned 968 to 1001); the Baphuon, built by Udayadityavarman II (reigned 1050 to 1066); and the Bayon, a Buddhist temple that was the most important structure erected by the great builder Jayavarman VII (reigned 1181 to about 1201). The latter reconstructed the Khmer capital after it had been captured and destroyed by the Chams (whose kingdom occupied what is now south-central Vietnam), who had used their fleet to launch a surprise attack.

Many of the other temples of Angkor were built to serve as foci for cults through which various important personages (kings who did not construct new temple mountains, members of the royal family, even a few members of the aristocracy) were identified with one of the gods of the Indian pantheon and thus assured immortality. The grandest such structure was Angkor Wat, which was built by Suryavarman II (ruled 1112 to 1152). He intended Angkor Wat as an architectural microcosm of the mythical world in which his remains were to be interred as a cultic expression of his identity with Vishnu.

Angkor's huge system of reservoirs, canals and moats served not only to provide water for irrigation, allowing intensive cultivation of areas surrounding the capital, but also as symbols of the great ocean which according to Hindu mythology surrounds Mt Meru.

According to the vivid account of Chou Ta-kuan, a Chinese commercial envoy who visited Angkor Thom in 1296, the city was at that time a magnificent and thriving metropolis. However, by the 13th century the vitality and power of the Khmer Empire were gradually declining. Jayavarman VII's unprecedented building campaign had exhausted his kingdom and Hinayana Buddhism, which was more restrained in its religious expression, was on the ascendancy. Meanwhile, the armies of the Thai king-

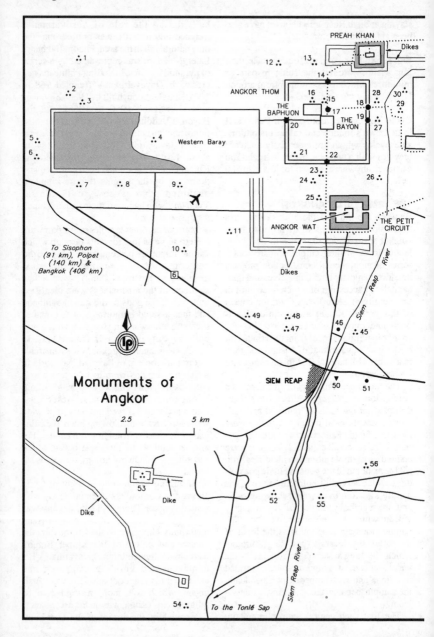

PREAH KHAN
Dikes

1
12
13
14
ANGKOR THOM
16
15
28
30
29
THE
BAPHUON
18
17
2
20
THE
19
BAYON
3
27
5
4
Western Baray
6
21
22
7
8
9
23
24
26
25
11
ANGKOR WAT
THE PETIT
CIRCUIT

To Sisophon
(91 km), Poipet
(140 km) &
Bangkok (406 km)

10

6

Dikes

49
48
47
46
45

Monuments of
Angkor

SIEM REAP
50
51

0   2.5   5 km

56

53
52
55

Dike

Dike

54

To the Tonlé Sap

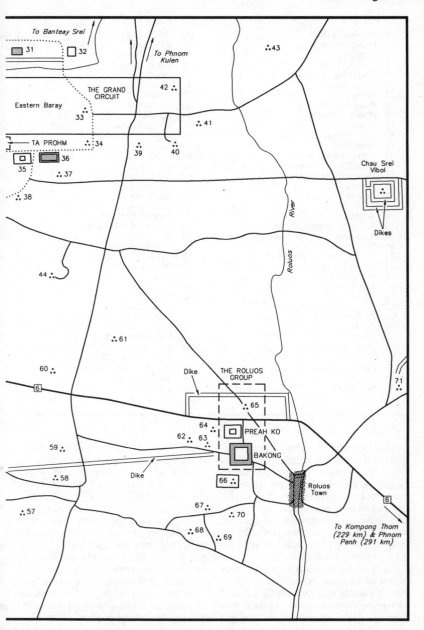

1	Prasat Kok Po	36	Sras Srang
2	Prasat Phnom Rung	37	Bat Chum
3	Prasat Roluh	38	Prasat Kravan
4	Western Mebon	39	Prasat Komnap
5	Prasat Trapeang Seng	40	Prei Prasat
6	Prei Kmeng	41	Banteay Samré
7	Ak Yom	42	Prasat To
8	Prasat Kas Ho	43	Phnom Bok
9	Prasat Ta Noreay	44	Kuk Bangro
10	Prasat Prei	45	Preah Einkosei
11	Prasat Trapeang Ropou	46	Angkor Conservation
12	Prasat Prei	47	Prasat Reach Kandal
13	Prasat Tonlé Snguot	48	Prasat Chak
14	North Gate of Angkor Thom	49	Prasat Patri
15	Terrace of Elephants	50	Bayon Chinese Restaurant
16	Phimeanakas	51	Central Market
17	Central Square of Angkor Thom	52	Vat Athvea
		53	Vat Chedei
18	Victory Gate	54	Phnom Krom
19	East Gate of Angkor Thom	55	Prasat Kuk O Chrung
20	West Gate of Angkor Thom	56	Prasat Rsei
21	Beng Thom	57	Prasat He Phka
22	South Gate of Angkor Thom	58	Prasat Kok Thlok
23	Baksei Chamkrong	59	Prasat Daun So
24	Phnom Bakheng	60	Tram Neak
25	Ta Prohm Kel	61	Kuk Taleh
26	Kapilapura	62	Prasat O Kaek
27	Chau Say Tevoda	63	Prasat Olok
28	Thommanon	64	Prasat Kandal Doeum
29	Ta Keo	65	Lolei
30	Ta Nei	66	Prasat Prei Monti
31	Preah Neak Pean	67	Svay Pream
32	Ta Som	68	Prasat Totoeng Thngai
33	Eastern Mebon	69	Prasat Trapeang Phong
34	Pre Rup	70	Kuk Dong
35	Banteay Kdei	71	Vat Bangro

doms in the west of the empire were beginning to threaten the Khmer heartland. In 1431 Thai armies captured and sacked Angkor, and the Khmer court dramatically abandoned the city, moving their capital eastward to a site near Phnom Penh. At this time, Hinayana Buddhist monks took over and preserved Angkor Wat, which before long became one of the most important pilgrimage sites in South-East Asia.

The 'lost city' of Angkor became the focus of intense European popular and scholarly interest after the publication in the 1860s of *Le Tour du Monde*, an account by the French naturalist Henri Mouhot of his voyages around the world. A group of talented and dedicated archaeologists and philologists, most of them French, soon undertook a comprehensive programme of research. Under the aegis of the École Française d'Extrême Orient, they began an arduous effort – begun in 1908 and interrupted at the beginning of the 1970s by the war – to clear away the jungle vegetation that was breaking apart the monuments and to rebuild the damaged structures, restoring them to something approaching their original grandeur. This work was carried out despite the complaints of some romantics, who preferred the mystery and romance imparted to the monuments by the thick jungle growth that was devouring them. As a response to the charges of this group, Ta Prohm Temple has been left in its wildly overgrown state.

Angkorian Monarchs

The following is a list of the kings who ruled the Khmer Empire from the 9th century to the 14th century:

King	Dates of Reign
Jayavarman II	802-850
Jayavarman III	850-877
Indravarman I	877-889
Yasovarman	889-910
Harshavarman I	910-?
Isanavarman II	?-928
Jayavarman IV	928-942
Harshavarman II	942-944
Rajendravarman	944-968
Jayavarman V	968-1001
Udayadityavarman	1001-1002
Suryavarman I	1002-1049
Udayadityavarman II	1049-1065
Harshavarman III	1065-1090
Jayavarman VI	1090-1108
Dharanindravarman I	1108-1112
Suryavarman II	1112-1152
Harshavarman IV	1152?
Dharanindravarman II	1152-1181
Jayavarman VII	1181-1201 (approx)
Indravarman II	1201-1243 (approx)
Jayavarman VIII	1243-1295
Sri-Indravarman	1295-1307
Sri-Indrajayavarman	1307-?
Jayavarman Paramesvara	mid-1300s

Chronology

According to the latest research, the chronology of the major monuments of Angkor is as follows:

Preah Ko (at Roluos)	879
Bakong (at Roluos)	881
Lolei (at Roluos)	900 (approx)
Eastern Mebon	952
Pre Rup	961
Banteay Srei	967
Ta Keo	1000 (approx)
Baphuon	1060 (approx)
Angkor Wat	1st half of 1100s
Ta Prohm	1186
Preah Khan	1191
Bayon & the walls & gates of Angkor Thom	end of 1100s

Information

Visitor Fees Each visitor to Angkor is charged a fee of US$120, which theoretically consists of a US$60 charge to visit Angkor Wat and an identical fee to visit the Bayon. I have no idea how much of this money, if any, goes towards the preservation of the monuments. Angry complaints by tourists have prompted the General Directorate of Tourism in Phnom Penh to try, unsuccessfully as yet, to convince Angkor Tourism to reduce the fee. You must pay the fee and obtain the permit before you can buy your flight ticket, and the permit can be checked in Angkor, often before you board the departing flight. Curiously, some people seem to be charged much less (typically US$15) and get away with it.

Organised Tours One-day tours to Angkor only give you a few hours to explore the ruins. They can be booked by tour agencies in Phnom Penh for around US$250; this includes the return flight, entry fees, guide and transport and lunch. Longer two-day, one-night tours cost US$350 to US$400; three days and two nights cost US$400 to US$450. The increasing flight frequency between Phnom Penh and Siem Reap makes tours easier to schedule but they are heavily booked.

What to See The three most magnificent temples at Angkor are the Bayon, which faces east and is best visited in the early morning; Ta Prohm, which is awesomely overgrown by the jungle; and Angkor Wat, which is the only monument here facing westward (it is at its finest in the late afternoon but also looks very impressive at sunrise). If you've got the time, all these monuments are well worth several visits each. Angkor's major sites can be seen without undue pressure in three full days of touring.

In the old days, visitors used to follow two circuits to the monuments in the vicinity of Angkor. The 17-km Petit Circuit began at Angkor Wat, headed northward to Phnom Bakheng, Baksei Chamkrong and Angkor

Thom (in which one visited the city wall and gates, the Bayon, the Baphuon, the Royal Enclosure, Phimeanakas, Preah Palilay, Tep Pranam, the Preah Pithu group, the Terrace of the Leper King, the Terrace of Elephants, the Central Square, the North Kleang, the South Kleang and the 12 Prasats Suor Prat), exited from Angkor Thom via Victory Gate (in the eastern wall), continued to Chau Say Tevoda, Thommanon, Spean Thma and Ta Keo, went north-east of the road to Ta Nei, turned southward to Ta Prohm, continued east to Banteay Kdei and the Sras Srang, and finally returned to Angkor Wat via Prasat Kravan.

The 26-km Grand Circuit began at Angkor Wat, exited Angkor Thom through the north gate, stopped at Preah Khan and Preah Neak Pean on its way eastward to Ta Som, then headed south via the Eastern Mebon to Pre Rup, whence it went westward and then south-westward back to Angkor Wat.

The Cambodian army has many hundreds of troops encamped around the monuments, and you're more likely to hear gunfire than the calls of jungle birds. Mines (including some with filament trip wires), laid either by the Khmer Rouge or to blow up Khmer Rouge infiltrators, continue to be a problem, and quite a number of local people are injured and killed each year. *Do not stray from well-marked paths* and, until the war ends, check with the army to make sure that the trails to where you're going have not been booby-trapped.

Guidebooks For a listing of some of the better guidebooks to Angkor, see the Facts for the Visitor chapter. *Henri Parmentier's Guide to Angkor* is readily available in Phnom Penh and may well be available in Siem Reap.

Maps Quite a number of excellent maps of the Angkor area have been published over the years. Angkor Tourism sells a good one reproduced from the Henri Parmentier guidebook. The May 1982 issue of *National Geographic* magazine has an excellent map showing Angkor in its prime.

Fauna The gibbons who used to live around Angkor have been shot by soldiers, for whom gibbon brain is a rare delicacy. Visitors should watch out for the dreaded Hanuman snake, a small but extremely venomous snake that can be instantly recognised by its bright light-green colour. Stinging red ants are another pest, but the bats that live in the temples are harmless. Keep an eye out for tree frogs. Between April and July, the jungle is often filled with the noise made by zillions of locust-like insects.

Flora Every gum tree around Angkor has a hole burnt into the base of the trunk. These are the result of the process by which resin, used for waterproofing boats, is extracted from the trees. Resin harvesters make a gash in the trunk and light a fire in it for a quarter of an hour or so. A week later, they return to take the resin that has collected.

THE PETIT CIRCUIT

In the old dispute about whether one should visit Angkor Wat or Angkor Thom first, my preference is for the latter. The order in which the monuments inside Angkor Thom are listed here makes for a nice circuit.

Angkor Thom

The fortified city of Angkor Thom, some 10 sq km in extent, was built in its present form by Angkor's greatest builder, Jayavarman VII (reigned 1181 to 1201), who came to power just after the disastrous sacking by the Chams of the previous Khmer capital, centred around the Baphuon. Angkor Thom, which may have had a million inhabitants (more than any European city of the period), is enclosed by a square wall eight metres high and 12 km in length and encircled by a moat 100 metres wide, said to have been inhabited by fierce crocodiles.

The city has five monumental gates, one each in the north, west and south walls and two in the east wall. The gates, which are 20 metres in height, are decorated to either side of the passageway with stone elephant trunks and crowned by four gargantuan faces of the

Top: Battle scene, the Bayon (TW)
Left: Battle scene, the Bayon (TW)
Right: Apsaras, the Bayon (TW)

Top Left: East Mebon (TW)
Top Right: Terrace of Elephants (TW)
Bottom Left: Terrace of the Leper King (TW)
Bottom Right: Angkor Thom - South Gate (TW)

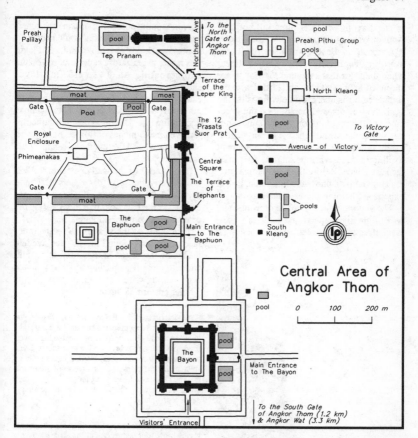

Central Area of Angkor Thom

bodhisattva Avalokitesvara facing the cardinal directions. In front of each gate, there stood giant statues of 54 gods (to the left of the causeway) and 54 demons (to the right of the causeway), a motif taken from the story of the Churning of the Ocean of Milk illustrated in the famous bas-relief at Angkor Wat. In the centre of the walled enclosure are the city's most important monuments, including the Bayon, the Baphuon, the Royal Enclosure, Phimeanakas and the Terrace of Elephants.

The Bayon The most outstanding feature of the Bayon, which was built by Jayavarman VII in the exact centre of the city of Angkor Thom, is the eerie and unsettling 3rd level, with its 49 towers projecting 172 icily smiling, gargantuan faces of Avalokitesvara. As you walk around, a dozen or more of the visages are visible at any one time – full-face or in profile, almost level with your eyes or peering down from on high – in an ever-changing phantasmagoria.

In addition, the Bayon is decorated with 1200 metres of extraordinary bas-reliefs incorporating over 11,000 figures. The famous carvings on the outer wall of the 1st level depict vivid scenes of everyday life in 12th century Cambodia.

The Bayon, which is three km north of Angkor Wat and 10 km from the Grand Hotel d'Angkor, is best visited in the early morning, especially shortly after dawn, when the trees that surround the Bayon are shrouded in mist and the air is filled with the sounds of birds and giant dew drops falling from the treetops and bursting on the vegetation of the jungle floor. As the sun comes up, sunlight first hits the tip of the central tower and then moves down the monument to illuminate, at various angles, face after face after face. Before the war, people used to camp out here under the full moon. Polish experts are helping preserve the Bayon.

The Bayon, which is made of sandstone, was originally planned and built as a two-level structure dedicated to the worship of

Tower, the Bayon

Shiva. At some point after its construction, it was decided that the Bayon would become a Mahayana Buddhist temple, and a 3rd level was rather haphazardly superimposed on the 2nd, creating an awkward 2nd level characterised by narrow courtyards, truncated galleries and stone panels facing each other only 60 cm apart. Some of the Buddhas decorating the Bayon were subsequently recarved into bunches of flowers or removed altogether when Hinduism was again in the ascendancy.

The interior of the wall enclosing the 2nd level is covered with bas-reliefs of Hindu myths. There are several rooms, empty except for the bats who live there, inside the central tower on the 3rd level.

Highlights of the bas-reliefs on the outer face of the wall around the 1st level include the following, listed in the order you would come to them if beginning at the south gate and walking with the wall to your left, as Khmer custom dictates:

A) On the first panel to the east of the south gate, you can see meals being prepared and served, a pig about to be dropped into a cauldron and, in the trees overhead, frolicking monkeys. In the next scene, Cham warriors (with headdresses) face off against Khmer soldiers. Farther along, there are scenes of two people playing chess, two boars being prodded to fight each other, women selling fish in the market and gossiping, and a cock fight.

B) About 1.5 metres east of the doorway a woman is giving birth; four metres east of the door, people are picking lice out of their hair; and six metres east of the door, Cham and Khmer ships are engaged in battle while below a crocodile and a pelican are each eating a fish. On the south wall in the south-east corner of the mural is a pirogue (a type of long canoe).

C) The first panel north of the south-east corner shows Hindus praying to a linga.

D) Just south of the east gate is a three-level panorama. On the 1st tier, Khmer soldiers march off to battle; notice the elephants and the ox carts, which are almost exactly like those still in use. The 2nd tier depicts the coffins of the dead being carried from the battlefield. In the centre of the 3rd tier, Jayavarman VII, shaded by parasols, is shown on horseback followed by legions of concubines (to the left).

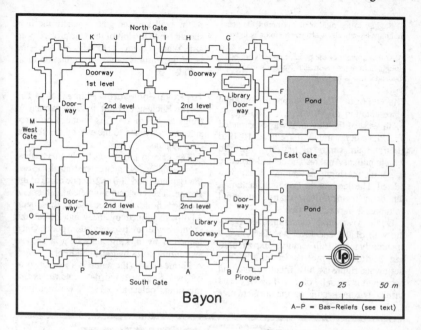

Bayon

North Gate

L K J I H G

Doorway   Doorway

1st level

Library

Doorway

West Gate

2nd level   2nd level

Door-way   Door-way

F   Pond

2nd level   2nd level

Door-way   Door-way

E

East Gate

Library

Doorway   Doorway

D   Pond

C

P   A   B   Pirogue

South Gate

0   25   50 m

A–P = Bas–Reliefs (see text)

E) The three-tiered battle scene here depicts Khmer troops (hatless and with slicked-back hair; on the left) facing Cham troops (on the right). On the lowest tier, dead and wounded soldiers are pictured at the feet of their marching comrades. In the middle of the scene, where the two armies meet, a Cham soldier (with a headdress) is cutting off a Khmer soldier's foot; at his feet is a severed head.

F) Another meeting of two armies. Notice the flag-bearers among the Cham troops (on the right). The Chams were defeated in the war depicted on panels D and E, which ended in 1181.

G) This panel shows the war of 1177, when the Khmers were defeated by the Chams and Angkor itself was pillaged. The wounded Khmer king is being lowered from the back of an elephant and a wounded Khmer general is being carried on a hammock suspended from a pole. Directly above, despairing Khmers are getting drunk. The Chams (on the right) are in hot pursuit of their vanquished enemy.

H) This badly deteriorated panel shows the Chams (on the left) chasing the Khmers.

I) The Cham armies are shown advancing.

J) On the lowest level of this unfinished three-tiered scene, the Cham armies are being defeated and expelled from the Khmer kingdom.

K) The two rivers, one next to the doorpost and the other three metres to the right, are teeming with fish.

L) At the western corner of the north wall is a Khmer circus. You can see a strong man holding three dwarfs and a man on his back spinning a wheel with his feet; above, there is a group of tightrope walkers. To the right of the circus, the royal court watches the goings on from a terrace, below which a procession of animals is marching. Some of the sculptures in this section remain unfinished.

M) At the far right of this panel, at the bottom, an antelope is being swallowed by a gargantuan fish. Among the smaller fish is a prawn.

N) A bit to the right of the centre of the 3rd tier (of four), the heads of two traitorous Khmer generals are being held aloft.

O) Slightly to the right of the centre of the panel, Brahmins have been chased up two trees by tigers.

P) At the far right of the panel, elephants are being brought in from the mountains. Nearby, a man with a bow and arrow is hunting.

The Baphuon The Baphuon, a pyramidal representation of Mt Meru, is 200 metres north-west of the Bayon. It was constructed by Udayadityavarman II (reigned 1050 to 1066) at the centre of his city, the third temple built at Angkor. The central structure is 43 metres high; its summit has disappeared. The decor of the Baphuon, including the door frames, lintels and octagonal columns, is particularly fine.

On the west side of the temple, the retaining wall of the 2nd level was fashioned – apparently in the 15th century – into a reclining Buddha 40 metres in length. The unfinished figure is a bit difficult to make out because it is partially obscured by vines and shrubs, but the head is on the northern side of the wall and the gate is where the hips should be; to the left of the gate protrudes an arm. When it comes to the legs and feet – the latter are entirely gone – imagination must suffice.

The Royal Enclosure & Phimeanakas The Royal Enclosure, built by Jayavarman V (reigned 968 to 1001) is bounded on three sides by walls and to the east by the Terrace of Elephants.

The gate to the Royal Enclosure nearest the Bayon is 150 metres east-north-east of the Baphuon and 200 metres due north of the Bayon. The enclosure, where innumerable wooden buildings once stood, has been wholly reclaimed by the jungle. Near the northern wall are two sandstone pools. Once bathed in by the king, they are now used as swimming holes by local children.

Phimeanakas (the name is a Khmer form of two Sanskrit words, *vimana akasa*, meaning 'celestial palace') was built by

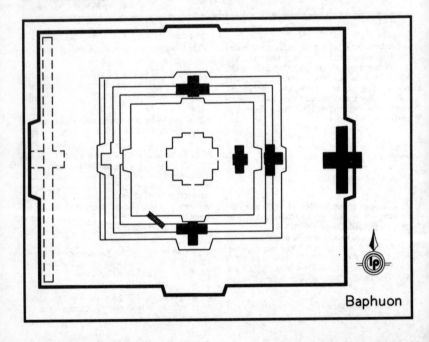

Baphuon

Rajendravarman (reigned 944 to 968), who returned the Khmer capital to Angkor from Koh Ker, 100 km to the north-east. It is at the intersection of the axes of Phnom Bakheng and the Eastern Baray. The temple, now in a dilapidated state, is a tri-level, pyramidal representation of Mt Meru. At one time, it had a sanctuary of light construction on top; the present chapel at the summit of Phimeanakas is of a later period. The staircase on the western side is in better condition than the other three.

Preah Palilay Preah Palilay, a rather deteriorated temple 200 metres north of the northern wall of the Royal Enclosure, was erected in its present form during the time of Jayavarman VII (reigned 1181 to 1201). It originally housed a Buddha, which has long since disappeared.

Tep Pranam Tep Pranam, an 82 by 34-metre cruciform Buddhist terrace 150 metres east of Preah Palilay, was once the base of a pagoda of lightweight construction. Nearby is a Buddha 4.5 metres in height; about 30 metres north of the Buddha is a small wooden monastery, home to six monks. Eight nuns live in the thatch buildings 40 metres north-east of the Buddha.

The Preah Pithu Group Preah Pithu, which is across the Northern Avenue from Tep Pranam, is a group of five 12th century Hindu and Buddhist temples enclosed by a wall.

The Terrace of the Leper King The Terrace of the Leper King, just north of the Terrace of Elephants, is a platform seven metres in height on top of which stands a nude, though sexless, statue (actually a copy – the original has been removed for safekeeping). The figure, possibly of Shiva, is believed by the locals to be of Yasovarman, founder of Angkor, who legend says died of leprosy. The front retaining walls are decorated with five or more tiers of meticulously executed carvings of seated *apsaras* (shapely dancing women); other figures include kings wearing pointed diadems, armed with short double-edged swords and accompanied by the court and princesses, who are adorned with rows of pearls. The terrace, built at the end of the 12th century, between the construction of Angkor Wat and that of the Bayon, once supported a pavilion made of lightweight materials.

On the south side of the Terrace of the Leper King (facing the Terrace of Elephants) there is an entryway to a long, narrow trench, excavated by archaeologists. This passageway follows the front wall of an earlier terrace that was covered up when the present structure was built. The four tiers of apsaras and other figures, including nagas (five, seven, nine or even 11-headed snakes), look as fresh as if they had been carved just yesterday.

The Terrace of Elephants The 350-metre-long Terrace of Elephants was used as a giant reviewing stand for public ceremonies and served as a base for the king's grand audience hall. As you stand here, try to imagine the pomp and grandeur of the Khmer Empire at its height, with infantry, cavalry, horse-drawn chariots and elephants parading across the Central Square in a colourful procession, pennants and standards aloft. Looking on is the god-king, a gold diadem on his head, shaded by multitiered parasols and attended by mandarins and handmaidens bearing gold and silver utensils.

The Terrace of Elephants has five outworks extending towards the Central Square, three in the centre and one at each end. The middle section of the retaining wall is decorated with life-size Garudas and lions; towards either end are the two parts of the famous parade of elephants.

The Kleangs & the 12 Prasats Suor Prat Along the east side of the Central Square are two groups of buildings, the North Kleang and the South Kleang, that may at one time have been palaces. The North Kleang dates from the period of Jayavarman V (reigned 968 to 1001).

Along the Central Square in front of the

two Kleangs are 12 laterite towers – 10 in a row and two more at right angles facing the Avenue of Victory – known as the Prasats Suor Prat. Archaeologists believe the towers, which form an honour guard of sorts along the Central Square, were constructed by Jayavarman VII (reigned 1181 to 1201). It is likely that each once contained either a linga or a statue.

Baksei Chamkrong

Located a bit south-west of the south gate of Angkor Thom, Baksei Chamkrong is one of the few brick edifices in the immediate vicinity of Angkor. It was once decorated with a covering of mortar of lime. Like virtually all the structures of Angkor, it opens to the east. In the early 10th century, Harshavarman I erected in this temple five statues: two of Shiva, one of Vishnu and two more of Devi.

Phnom Bakheng

Phnom Bakheng, also known as Indradri (Mountain of Indra), served as the temple mountain of the first city of Angkor, Yasodharapura, the capital built by Yasovarman (reigned 889 to 910). This 65-metre-high hill, 400 metres south of the south gate of Angkor Thom, offers a panoramic view of Angkor Thom, Angkor Wat and surrounding areas. The view is best just before sunset. The summit could once be reached by four staircases; today, the northern one is in the best condition. There is also a path up the hill.

Angkor Wat

Angkor Wat, with its soaring towers and extraordinary bas-reliefs, is considered by many to be one of the most inspired and spectacular monuments ever conceived by the human mind. It was built by Suryavarman II (reigned 1112 to 1152) to honour Vishnu (with whom he, as god-king, was identified) and for later use as his funerary temple. Angkor Wat, which is 6.4 km north

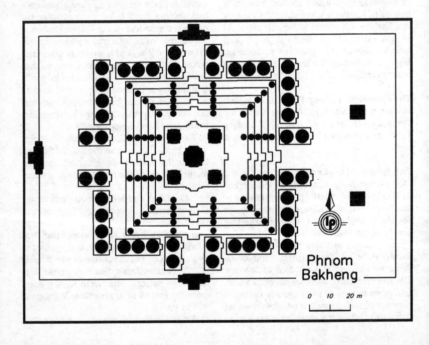

Phnom Bakheng

0   10   20 m

of the Grand Hotel d'Angkor, is the only monument in the area that faces westward. There is a refreshment stand opposite the main entrance.

After the Khmers moved their capital to the Phnom Penh area in the mid-15th century, Angkor Wat was inhabited by Buddhist monks, who protected the monument from pillage and the ravages of encroaching vegetation. Today, there are two pagodas inside the complex – one south of the main temple and the other north-west of it; about 20 monks live at Angkor Wat. Indian archaeologists are helping to preserve the temple.

Angkor Wat is surrounded by a moat, 190 metres wide, that forms a giant rectangle measuring 1.5 by 1.3 km. From the west, a laterite causeway crosses the moat; the holes in the paving stones held wooden pegs that were used to lift and position the stones during construction, after which the pegs were sawed off. The sandstone blocks from which Angkor Wat was built were apparently quarried many km away (perhaps at Phnom Kulen) and floated down the Siem Reap River on rafts.

The rectangular wall around the enclosure, which measures 1025 by 800 metres, has a gate in each side, but the main entrance, a 235-metre-wide porch richly decorated with carvings and sculptures, is on the western side. In the gate tower to the right as you approach is a statue of Vishnu, 3.25 metres in height, hewn from a single block of sandstone; its eight arms hold a mace, a spear, a disk, a conch shell and other items. The locks of hair you see lying about have

been cut off as an offering either by young women and men preparing to get married or by people who seek to give thanks for their good fortune (such as having recovered from an illness).

An avenue, 475 metres long and 9.5 metres wide and lined with naga balustrades, leads from the main entrance to the central temple, passing between two graceful galleries – perhaps libraries – and then two pools.

The central temple complex consists of three storeys, each of which encloses a square surrounded by intricately interlinked galleries. The corners of the 2nd and 3rd storeys are marked by towers topped with pointed cupolas. Rising 31 metres above the 3rd level and 55 metres above the ground is the central tower, which gives the whole ensemble its sublime unity. At one time, the central sanctuary of Angkor Wat held a gold statue of Vishnu mounted on a winged Garuda that represented the deified god-king Suryavarman II.

Stretching around the outside of the central temple complex, which is enclosed by an esplanade framed by a naga balustrade, is an 800-metre-long series of extraordinary bas-reliefs. The carvings were once sheltered by the cloister's wooden roof, which long ago rotted away (except for one original beam in the western half of the northern gallery; the other roofed sections are reconstructions). The following is a brief description of the epic events depicted on the panels, which are listed in the order in which you'll come to them if you walk beginning on the west side and keeping the bas-reliefs

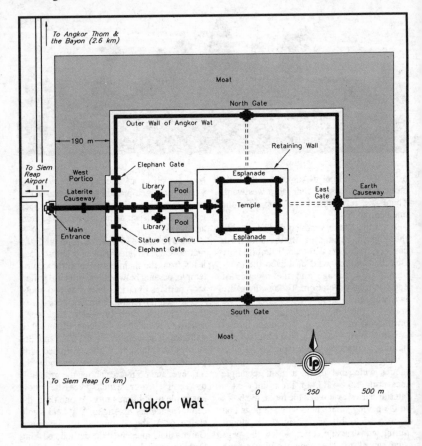

Angkor Wat

to your left (as is proper according to Khmer tradition):

A) The southern portion of the west gallery depicts a battle scene from the Hindu Mahabarata epic in which the Kauravas (coming from the north) and the Pandavas (coming from the south) advance in serried ranks towards each other, meeting in furious battle. Infantry are shown on the lowest tier, officers on elephant-back and chiefs on the 2nd and 3rd tiers. Among the more interesting details (from left to right): a dead chief lying on a pile of arrows and surrounded by his grieving parents and troops; a warrior on an elephant who has, by putting down his weapon, accepted defeat; and a mortally wounded officer, falling from the conveyance in which he is riding into the arms of his soldiers. Over the centuries, some sections have been polished by millions of hands to look like black marble.

The portico at the south-west corner is decorated with sculptures representing subjects taken from the Ramayana.

B) The remarkable western section of the south gallery depicts scenes from Khmer history; it includes inscriptions identifying the people pictured. In the south-west corner about two metres from the floor is Suryavarman II mounted on an elephant, wearing the royal tiara and armed with a battle-axe; he is shaded by 15 umbrellas and fanned by legions of servants. Farther on is a procession of well-armed soldiers and officers on horseback; among them march elephants

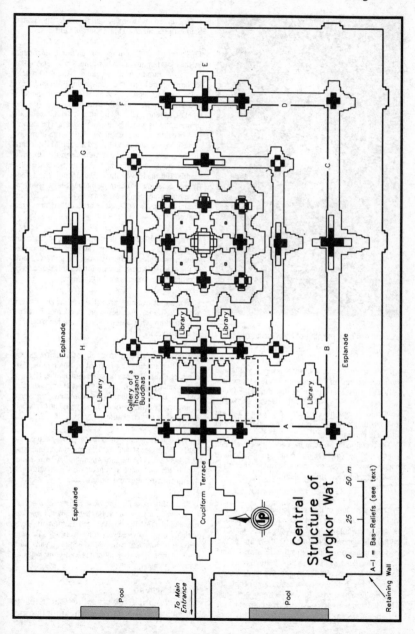

Central
Structure of
Angkor Wat

0   25   50 m

A–I = Bas-Reliefs (see text)

Detail of The Churning of the Ocean of Milk

sions, served by women, children and attendants; below, the condemned suffer horrible tortures.

D) The south section of the east gallery is decorated by the most famous of the bas-relief scenes at Angkor Wat, the Churning of the Ocean of Milk (in French: le Barattage de l'Océan de Lait). This brilliantly executed carving depicts 88 Asuras (devils; on the left) and 92 Devas (gods) with crested helmets (on the right), churning up the sea in order to extract the elixir of immortality, which both groups covet. The extraction is being accomplished by rotating the immense serpent Vasuki, who is entwined around Mt Mandara (in the centre, resting on a turtle). Vishnu, on the side of the mountain, is assisting the whole process; on top stands Indra, surveying the proceedings. Other figures watching the churning include Shiva, Brahma, the monkey-god Hanuman and many agitated fish and sea-monsters. Above, Apsaras gracefully dance in the heavens.

E) This gate, which has no stairs leading up to it, was used by the king and others for mounting and dismounting elephants directly from the gallery. North of the gate is a Khmer inscription recording the erection of a nearby stupa in the 18th century.

F) The unfinished northern section of the east gallery shows a furious and desperate encounter between Vishnu, riding on a Garuda, and innumerable demons (the Danavas).

G) The unfinished eastern section of the north gallery shows Krishna arriving in front of Sonitapura, residence of Bana, who has ravished Aniruddha. His way is blocked by a wall of fire, which is extinguished by Garuda. Bana is defeated and captured, but Shiva (haloed and bearing a trident) intervenes on his behalf and Krishna spares his life.

H) The western section of the north gallery depicts the battle of the Devas and the Daityas, which ends in a duel between Vishnu and Kalameni. All the major gods of the Brahmanic pantheon are shown with their traditional attributes and mounts.

I) The northern half of the west gallery show scenes from the Ramayana. In the Battle of Lanka, Rama (on the shoulders of the monkey-god Hanuman), along with his army of monkeys, battles 10-headed Ravana, seducer of Rama's beautiful wife Sita. Ravana rides on a chariot drawn by monsters and commands an army of giants.

carrying their chiefs, whose bearing is bold and warlike. Just west of the vestibule is the rather disorderly Thai mercenary army, at that time allied with the Khmers in their conflict with the Chams. While the Khmer troops have square breastplates and are armed with spears, the Thais wear headdresses and skirts and carry tridents.

The rectangular holes in the carving were created when, long ago, pieces of the scene – reputed to have magical powers – were removed. Part of this panel was damaged by an artillery shell in 1971.

C) The eastern half of the south gallery, the ceiling of which was restored in the 1930s, depicts the punishments and rewards of the 37 heavens and 32 hells. On the left, the upper and middle tiers show fine gentlemen and ladies proceeding towards 18-armed Yama, judge of the dead, seated on a bull; below him are his assistants, Dharma and Sitragupta. On the lower tier is the road to hell, along which wicked people are being dragged by devils. To Yama's right, the tableau is divided into two parts separated by a horizontal line of Garudas: above, the elect dwell in beautiful man-

Prasat Kravan

The five brick towers of Prasat Kravan, which are arranged in a north-south line and oriented to the east, were built for Hindu worship in 921. It's unusual in that it was not constructed by royalty and this accounts for its slightly remote location, away from the centre of the capital. Prasat Kravan is just south of the road between Angkor Wat and Banteay Kdei.

The group was partially restored in 1968 and is notable for the bas-reliefs cut into the bricks on the interior walls. The images in the largest central tower show eight-armed Vishnu on the back wall, taking the three gigantic steps with which he reclaimed the world on the left wall and riding the Garuda on the right wall. The northernmost of the towers has reliefs of Vishnu's consort, Lakshmi.

One of Vishnu's best loved incarnations was as the dwarf Vamana who reclaimed the world from the demon-king Bali. The dwarf politely asked the demon for a patch of ground upon which to meditate, saying that the patch need only be big enough that he, the dwarf, could walk across it in three paces. The demon agreed, only to see the dwarf swell into a giant who strode across the universe in three mighty steps. From this legend Vishnu is sometimes known as the 'long strider'.

Banteay Kdei & the Sras Srang

Banteay Kdei, a massive Buddhist temple of the second half of the 12th century, is surrounded by four concentric walls. The outer wall measures 500 by 700 metres; each of its four entrances is decorated with Garudas and holds aloft one of Jayavarman VII's favourite themes, the four visages of Avalokitesvara. The inside of the central tower was never finished.

Just east of Banteay Kdei is a basin of earlier construction, Sras Srang (Pool of Ablutions), measuring 800 by 400 metres. A tiny island in the middle once bore a wooden temple, of which only the stone base remains.

There is a mass grave of hundreds of victims of the Khmer Rouge a bit north of Sras Srang on the other side of the road. It is marked by a wooden memorial.

Lion, Sras Srang

Ta Prohm

Ta Phrom was built as a Buddhist temple during the 12th century. In the late 12th century, under Jayavarman VII, 18 high priests and 2740 ordinary priests officiated here. Of the 12,640 people entitled to lodgings within the enclosure, 615 were choristers who participated in the rituals.

One of the largest Khmer edifices of the Angkorian period, Ta Prohm has been left just as it looked when the first French explorers set eyes on it over a century ago. Whereas the other major monuments of Angkor have been preserved and made suitable for scholarly research by a massive programme to clear away the all-devouring jungle, this Buddhist temple has been left to its fate of inexorable, arboreous ruination. Ta Prohm, its friezes enmeshed in tendrilous nets, its stones slowly being pried asunder by the roots of the huge trees rising from its galler-

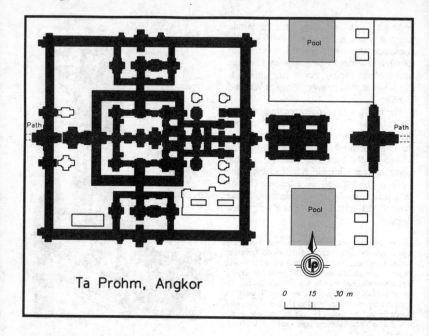

Ta Prohm, Angkor

0   15   30 m

ies and towers, stands as a monument to the awesome fecundity and power of the jungle. It is not to be missed.

Courtyards and cloisters are impassable, clogged with jumbled piles of delicately carved stone blocks dislodged by the roots of long-decayed trees. Bas-reliefs on bulging walls are carpeted by a dozen different kinds of lichens, mosses and creeping plants, and shrubs sprout from the roofs of monumental porches. Trees, hundreds of years old – some supported by flying buttresses – tower overhead, their leaves filtering the sunlight and casting a greenish pall over the whole scene.

More than the rustling of leaves accompanies the visitor to Ta Prohm: birds chatter invisibly overhead and crickets chirp to each other among the mimosa plants; nearby, butterflies flutter about silently and giant spiders noiselessly stalk their prey. Occasionally, you glimpse a tree frog hopping from one fallen lintel to another or a bat flying erratically towards its refuge in some dark, tomblike recess of the temple. Inaudible over the jungle noises are the munch-munch-munch of termites and the march of stinging red ants in search of food. And all the while, unseen, the bright-green Hanuman snake slithers silently, stealthily between the stones.

The mystery of the jungle mingles with the mystery of the ancient galleries and halls. Scenes of Indiana Jones making some near escape from the Temple of Doom may spring to mind, bringing to consciousness the nightmarish thought that somehow, the jungle will reach out and grab you, twisting its vines around your neck just as it has done to the apsaras lying corpselike nearby.

Visitors may want to equip themselves with a compass. There are narrow, overgrown paths into the complex from the east and the west.

Ta Keo

Ta Keo, built by Jayavarman V (reigned 968

to 1001), was dedicated to the worship of Shiva and was the first Angkorian monument constructed entirely in sandstone. The summit of the central tower, which is surrounded by four lower towers, is over 50 metres high. This quincunx arrangement with four towers at the corners of a square and a fifth tower in the centre is typical of many Angkor 'temple mountains'. The process of decorating Ta Keo's particularly hard sandstone was never completed and the temple has a spartan and bare feeling compared to the almost baroque decoration of other Angkor monuments.

Ta Nei

Ta Nei, 800 metres north of Ta Keo near the north-west corner of the Eastern Baray, was built by Jayavarman VII (reigned 1181 to 1201).

Spean Thma

The bridge of Spean Thma (the name means stone bridge), of which an arch and several piers remain, is 200 metres east of Thommanon. It was one of the latest structures constructed by the last great builder of Angkor, Jayavarman VII and is the only large bridge in the vicinity of Angkor of

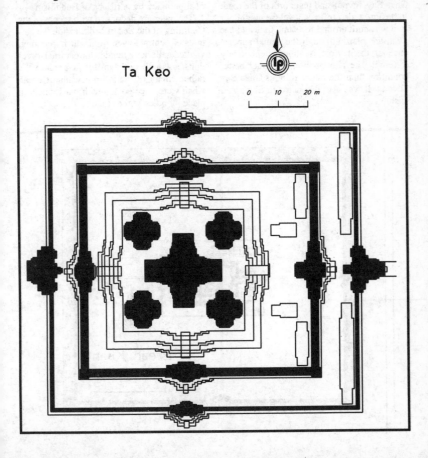

Ta Keo

0 10 20 m

which anything remains. Just north of the bridge is a large and surprisingly elegant water wheel.

Chau Say Tevoda

Just east of the Victory Gate on the east side of Angkor Thom, the Chau Say Tevoda is immediately south of the road. It was probably built during the second quarter of the 12th century and dedicated to Shiva and Vishnu.

Thommanon

The Thommanon Temple is just north of the Chau Say Tevoda and just north of the road. In design it also reflects its close neighbour as it was built around the same time and has a similar plan, although the actual appearance of the temple is almost deliberately different. The Thommanon is in much better condition than the rather ruinous Chau Say Tevoda. It was also dedicated to Shiva and Vishnu.

THE GRAND CIRCUIT
Preah Khan

The great temple of Preah Khan (Sacred Sword), which is three km from the Bayon and about 1.5 km north-east of the northern gate of Angkor Thom, was built by Jayavarman VII in the late 12th century. This rarely visited monument, which is surrounded by four concentric walls, is in an excellent state of preservation, though since 1972 the area has become overgrown by vines and young trees. Most of the friezes and carvings, which depict Hindu epics and deities, were systematically effaced centuries ago in an assertion of supremacy by partisans of Buddhism.

The gates are decorated with scenes of the Churning of the Sea of Milk. Inside the bat-infested central tower, from which four long, vaulted galleries extend in the cardinal directions, is a tomb, perhaps of Jayavarman VII's father. Many of the interior walls of Preah Khan were once coated with plaster held in place by holes in the stone.

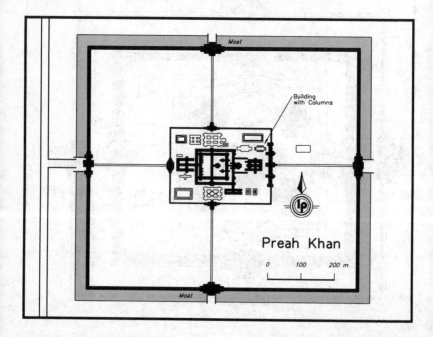

If you've come to this very extensive temple with a car and driver, you can ask to be dropped off at the west entrance gate and have the vehicle go round to the north entrance gate and wait for you there. A particular curiosity is the two-storey building near the east entrance. The round columns give it an almost Mediterranean feel, although it is probable that they are simply an imitation of the wooden architecture of the period. Preah Khan's isolation, sprawling design and somewhat overgrown appearance make it a very satisfying temple to visit.

Just north of Preah Khan is Banteay Prei, which dates from the same period.

Preah Neak Pean

The late 12th century Buddhist temple of Preah Neak Pean (Intertwined Naga), which was built by Jayavarman VII (ruled 1181 to 1201), consists of a square pool with four smaller square pools arranged on each axis. In the centre of the large central pool is a circular 'island' encircled by the two nagas (snakes) whose intertwined tails give the temple its name. Although it has been many centuries since the pools were last filled with water, it's easy for a modern visitor to envisage the complex as a huge swim-up bar at some fancy hotel.

In the pool around the central island there were once four statues but only one remains, reconstructed from the debris by the French archaeologists who cleared the site. The curious figure has the body of a horse supported by a tangle of human legs. It relates to a legend that Avalokitesvara once saved a group of shipwrecked followers from an island of ghouls by transforming himself into a flying horse.

Water once flowed from the central pool into the four peripheral pools via ornamental spouts which can still be seen in the pavilions at each axis of the pool. The spouts are in the form of an elephant's head, a horse's head, a lion's head and a human head. The pool was

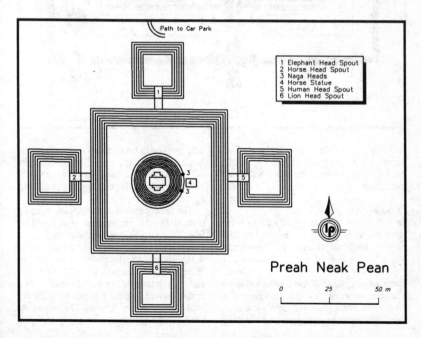

Path to Car Park

1 Elephant Head Spout
2 Horse Head Spout
3 Naga Heads
4 Horse Statue
5 Human Head Spout
6 Lion Head Spout

Preah Neak Pean

0   25   50 m

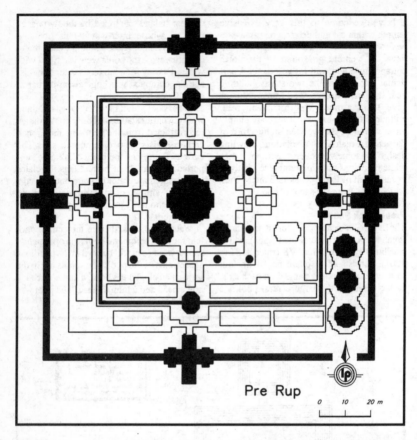

Pre Rup

0   10   20 m

used for rites of ritual purification and the complex was originally in the centre of a huge three by 0.9-km lake, now dried up and overgrown.

Ta Som

Ta Som, which stands to the east of Preah Neak Pean, is yet another of the late 12th century Buddhist temples of Jayavarman VII. Much of Ta Som is in a ruined state.

The Eastern Baray & the Eastern Mebon

The enormous one-time reservoir known as the Eastern Baray (Baray Oriental) was excavated by Yasovarman (reigned 889 to 910),

who marked its four corners with steles. This basin, the most important of the public works of Yasodharapura, Yasovarman's capital, is seven by 1.8 km. It was fed by the Siem Reap River.

The temple known as the Eastern Mebon, erected by Rajendravarman (ruled 944 to 968), is on an islet in the centre of the Eastern Baray. This Hindu temple is very similar in design though smaller in size to the Pre Rup Temple, which was built 15 to 20 years later and lies immediately to the south. The temple mountain form is surmounted by the usual quincunx of towers. The elaborate brick shrines are dotted with neatly arranged holes which have given some observers the idea that they were once covered in metal plates. In fact, the towers were covered in plaster. The base of the temple is guarded at its corner by stone figures of harnessed elephants, some of which are still in a reasonable state of preservation.

Pre Rup

Pre Rup, built by Rajendravarman (ruled 944 to 968), is about 1.5 km south of the Eastern Mebon. Like its nearby predecessor, the temple consists of a pyramid-shaped temple mountain with the uppermost of the three tiers carrying five square-shaped shrines arranged as a quincunx. Also like the Eastern Mebon, the brick sanctuaries were once decorated with a plaster coating, fragments of which remain on the south-west tower. There are some fine lintel carvings here.

Pre rup means 'turning the body' and refers to a traditional method of cremation in which the corpse's outline is traced in the cinders, first in one direction and then in the other. A legendary cremation is said to have taken place at this spot.

OTHER AREAS

The Western Baray

The Western Baray (Baray Occidental), measuring eight by 2.3 km, was excavated to provide water for the intensive cultivation of lands around Angkor. In the centre of the basin is the Western Mebon, where the giant bronze statue of Vishnu, now in the National Museum in Phnom Penh, was found. It is accessible by boat.

Phnom Krom

The temple of Phnom Krom, which is 12 km south of Siem Reap on a hill overlooking the Tonlé Sap, dates from the 11th century. The three towers, dedicated (from north to south) to Vishnu, Shiva and Brahma, are in a ruined state. The ferry from Phnom Penh and Kompong Chhnang docks near here.

Banteay Samré

Banteay Samré, 400 metres east of the southeast corner of the Eastern Baray, was built in the third quarter of the 12th century. It consists of a central temple with four wings preceded by a hall and accompanied by two

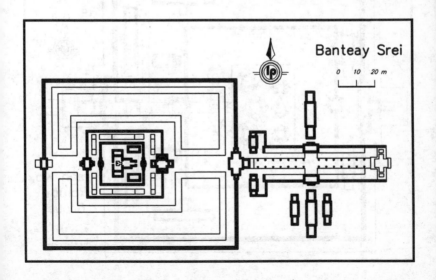

Banteay Srei

0   10   20 m

libraries, the southern one of which is remarkably well preserved. The ensemble is enclosed by two concentric walls.

The road to Banteay Samré should only be attempted in vehicles with high ground clearance.

Banteay Srei

Banteay Srei, which is 21 km north-east of the Bayon and eight km west of Phnom Kulen, was built by Jayavarman V (ruled 968 to 1001) and dedicated to Shiva. This large and privately built monument, considered by many to be the most perfect of Khmer temples, is famous for its exquisite carvings executed in pink sandstone and for its inventive architecture. The gate-pavilions are particularly fine.

You need a vehicle with plenty of ground clearance to attempt the rough road to Banteay Srei.

Phnom Kulen

The sheer walls of Phnom Kulen, which is some 28 km north-east of the Bayon, rise to an elevation of 461 metres.

Beng Mealea

The 12th century temple of Beng Mealea is about 40 km east of the Bayon (as the crow flies) and 6.5 km south-east of Phnom Kulen. Its ruined state is probably the result of civil strife or wars with the Thais. Beng Mealea is enclosed by a moat measuring 1200 by 900 metres.

THE ROLUOS GROUP

The monuments of Roluos, which served as the capital of Indravarman I (reigned 877 to 889), are among the earliest large, permanent temples built by the Khmers and mark the beginning of Khmer classical art. Before the construction of Roluos, only lighter (and non-durable) construction materials had been employed, even for religious structures.

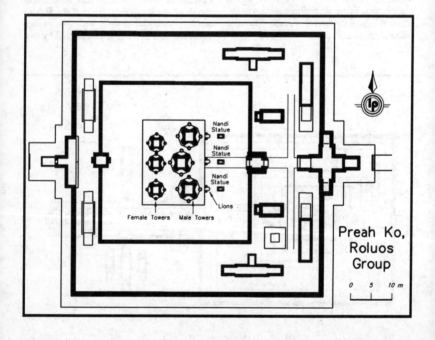

Preah Ko, Roluos Group

0   5   10 m

Preah Ko

Preah Ko was erected by Indravarman I in the late 9th century. The six brick towers *(prasats)*, aligned in two rows and decorated with carved sandstone and plaster reliefs, face eastward; the central tower of the front row is larger than the others. There are inscriptions in Sanskrit on the doorposts of each temple.

The temples of Preah Ko (Sacred Oxen, so named for the three Nandi statues that stand in front of the first row of temples) were dedicated by Indravarman I to his deified ancestors on 29 January 880. The front towers relate to male ancestors or gods, the rear towers to female ancestors or goddesses. Lions guard the steps up to the temple platform.

Bakong

Bakong, which was built and dedicated to Shiva by Indravarman I, played the same role for his capital of Hariharalaya as did Phnom Bakheng for Yasovarman's Angkor. That is, it was built as a representation of Mt Meru and as such served as the city's central temple. The eastward-facing complex consists of a five-tier central pyramid of sandstone, 60 metres square at the base, flanked by eight towers (or what's left of them) of brick and sandstone and by other minor sanctuaries. Several of the eight towers down below are still partly covered by their original plasterwork.

The complex is enclosed by three concentric walls and a broad moat. Note the stone elephants on each corner of the first three levels of the central temple. There are 12 stupas – four to a side – on the 3rd tier. The sanctuary on the 5th level was added at a later stage. There is a modern Buddhist monastery at the north-east corner of the area between the middle and inner walls.

Lolei

The four brick towers of Lolei, which are an

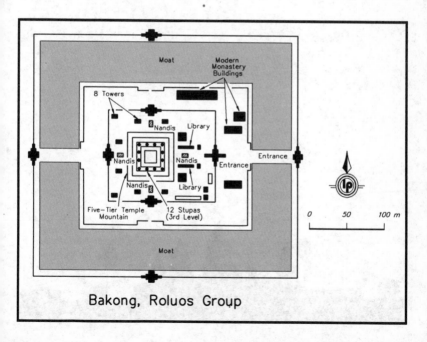

Bakong, Roluos Group

almost exact replica of the towers of Preah Ko although in much worse shape, were built on an islet in the centre of a large reservoir – now rice fields – by Yasovarman (ruled 889 to 910), the founder of the first city at Angkor. The sandstone carvings in the niches of the temples are worth a look and there are Sanskrit inscriptions on the door-posts. According to one of the inscriptions, the four towers were dedicated by Yasovarman to his mother, his father and his grandparents on his mother's side on 12 July 893.

Getting There & Away

The Roluos Group is 13 km east of Siem Reap along National Route 6. Preah Ko is 600 metres south of National Route 6 (to the right as you head away from Siem Reap); Bakong is 1.5 km south of National Route 6.

To get to Lolei from the turn-off to Preah Ko and Bakong, continue eastward for 400 metres, turn left (north-westward) and continue for half a km. There are modern-day Buddhist monasteries at Bakong and Lolei.

Around Cambodia

The South Coast

KAMPOT កំពត
The pretty riverine town of Kampot (population 14,000) is on the Tuk Chhou River, also called the Prek Thom River, five km from the sea. Although many buildings in town were damaged by the Khmer Rouge, Kampot retains much of its charm. There are plans to develop an infrastructure for tourism here.

Durian haters beware: Kampot Province is Cambodia's most important durian producing region.

Information
Post The GPO is along the river near the Kampot Province Hotel. There is supposed to be a telephone link between Kampot and Phnom Penh.

To Chu Falls
The To Chu Falls are just north of Kampot towards the hills.

Places to Stay & Eat
Hotels include the *Phnom Kamchai Hotel* and the *Phnom Khieu Hotel* (Blue Mountain Hotel) near the central plaza and the *Kampot Province Hotel* on the river.

There are food stalls in the main market and elsewhere around town.

Getting There & Away
The 148-km drive from Phnom Penh to Kampot along National Route 3 now takes five hours because of the road's dilapidated state (25 years ago it took only 2½ hours). The roads around Kampot are in extremely poor condition.

BOKOR HILL STATION ស្ថានីយភ្នំបូកគោ
The mountaintop hill station of Bokor (elevation 1080 metres) is famous for its pleasant climate, rushing streams, forested vistas and stunning panoramas of the sea. The best time of year to visit Bokor, which is in the Elephant Mountains, is between November and May.

There are plans to redevelop Bokor, which has been virtually abandoned since the mid-1970s.

Getting There & Away
Bokor is 41 km from Kampot and 190 km from Phnom Penh. The access road is in very bad condition.

POPOKVIL FALLS ទឹកជ្រោះពពកវិល
The two waterfalls of Popokvil, 14 and 18 metres high, are not far from the access road to Bokor Hill Station.

KEP កែប
The seaside resort of Kep (Kep-sur-Mer), with its six-km palm-shaded corniche, was once a favourite vacation spot for Cambodia's French-influenced elite, who flocked here to enjoy such pursuits as yachting, gambling, fishing, water skiing and skin diving. Under the Khmer Rouge, the town (founded in 1908) and its many villas were completely destroyed – not neglected and left to decay, but intentionally turned into utter ruins. The Khmer Rouge also turned the underground petrol tank of the old Shell station into a mass grave. By 1979, not a single building remained intact in Kep.

Although there are plans to rebuild Kep and re-establish it as a beach resort, at present it is a ghost town with no hotels or other tourist facilities.

Kep is subject to the south-west monsoon. The best time of year to visit Kep is from the end of October to the end of June.

Getting There & Away
If you take the train, get off at the Damnak Chang Aeu Railway Station, which is a few km from Kep. By road, Kep is 24 km south-

east of Kampot and 49 km from the Vietnamese town of Ha Tien. There is a border crossing eight km north of Ha Tien, but it is not presently open for foreigners.

KIRIROM គីរីរម្យ

The hill station of Kirirom, set amid pine forests 675 metres above sea level, is 112 km south-west of Phnom Penh. It is in the Elephant Mountains to the west of National Route 4.

KOMPONG SOM កំពង់សោម

Kompong Som (formerly Sihanoukville), Cambodia's only maritime port, had a population of 16,000 in the mid-1960s and probably has the same population now. Near town there are superb beaches and, for skin-diving enthusiasts, shoals and reefs teeming with multicoloured fish.

Ream

The town of Ream, the country's most important harbour on the Gulf of Thailand before the construction of Kompong Son, is at the southern tip of the Kompong Som Peninsula.

Getting There & Away

Kompong Som is 232 km from Phnom Penh via one of the best roads in the country, National Route 4. When the rail line is open, Kompong Som can also be reached from the capital by train. The road from Kampot to Kompong Som is in very bad condition.

A Soviet-built airfield near Kompong Som opened in late 1983.

KOH KONG កោះកុង

The beautiful island of Koh Kong, in the Gulf of Thailand, just off the western coast of Koh Kong Province, is only a few dozen km from Thailand and has become a centre for smuggling Thai and Singaporean consumer goods into Cambodia. There are plans to develop tourism on Koh Kong, which is only 80 km south-east of Thailand's island of Ko Chang.

Koh Kong Province, which like neighbouring Kampot Province is blessed

with innumerable offshore islands of all sizes, can be reached by chartered plane from Phnom Penh and by boat from Kompong Som.

Central Cambodia

KOMPONG CHHNANG កំពង់ឆ្នាំង

Kompong Chhnang (population 15,000) is an important fishing and transportation centre on the Tonlé Sap. The area is known for its pottery.

Getting There & Away

Land distances from Kompong Chhnang:

Phnom Penh	90 km
Battambang	185 km
Poipet (Thai border)	331 km
Pursat	97 km
Sisophon	282 km

Kompong Chhnang is served by riverboats departing from the Psar Cha Ministry of Transport Ferry Landing in the capital. The ferries leave Phnom Penh at 8 am and arrive in Kompong Chhnang around 4 pm.

PURSAT

The provincial capital of Pursat had a population of 16,000 in the mid-1960s.

Getting There & Away

Land distances from Pursat:

Phnom Penh	187 km
Battambang	105 km
Kompong Chhnang	202 km
Poipet (Thai border)	234 km
Sisophon	185 km

Pursat is on the Phnom Penh-Battambang railway line.

KOMPONG CHAM កំពង់ចាម

Archaeological sites around Kompong Cham (population 30,000 in the mid-1960s) include the following:

1) Wat Nokor (two km from town), an 11th century Mahayana Buddhist shrine of sandstone and laterite, was reconsecrated for Hinayana worship in the 15th century.

2) The hills of Phnom Pros and Phnom Srei (35 km north-west of town) offer superb views of the area. At the base of Phnom Pros there are five mass graves in which thousands of people killed by the Khmer Rouge were buried.

3) Preah Theat Preah Srei (south of Kompong Cham), capital of Chenla during the 8th century, was seized by a Srivijayan (Sumatran) fleet in 802.

4) Prey Nokor (38 km from town), to the south-east, was a Khmer capital during the 6th or 7th centuries. The outer wall encloses a vast area at the centre of which are two square sanctuaries.

There are a number of rubber plantations in the vicinity of Kompong Cham, including Cham Car Leur to the north of the city and the 7-1 Plantation (formerly known as Chup), which is east of the city. Bulgaria and the USSR have provided assistance to increase rubber production in this area.

Getting There & Away

By road, Kompong Cham is 144 km from Phnom Penh. Take National Route 5 north from the capital, cross the Tonlé Sap River at Prek Kdam Ferry (32 km north of Phnom Penh) and go north-eastward on National Route 6. At Skun, continue eastward on National Route 7.

The ferry ride from Phnom Penh to Kompong Cham is either an all-day affair or a 24-hour trip (with an overnight stay in Prek Por), depending on which boat you take. See the Getting There & Away section in the Phnom Penh chapter for more information.

KOMPONG THOM កំពង់ធំ

The road north from Kompong Thom leads to a number of interesting archaeological sites, including Sambor Prei Kuk, Preah Khan, Melou Prey, Preah Vihear and Ko Ker; details are listed in the following sections. Phnom Santuk, which is west of Kompong

Thom, consists of a number of ruined brick sanctuaries.

Getting There & Away

Land distances from Kompong Thom:

Phnom Penh	165 km
Poipet	298 km
Siem Reap	146 km
Sisophon	249 km

SAMBOR PREI KUK សំបូរព្រៃគុក

Sambor Prei Kuk (also known as Isanapura), which is 35 km north of Kompong Thom, was the capital of Chenla during the reign of the early 7th century king Isanavarman. It is the most impressive group of pre-9th century monuments in Cambodia. The site consists of three groups of edifices, most of which are made of brick, whose design prefigures a number of later developments in Khmer art. Sambor Prei Kuk continued to be an important centre of scholarship during the Angkorian period.

PREAH KHAN ព្រះខ័ន

The vast laterite and sandstone temple of Preah Khan, originally dedicated to Hindu deities, was reconsecrated to Buddhist worship in the early 11th century. Nearby monuments include Preah Damrei, guarded by massive elephants; Preah Thkol, a cruciform shrine two km east of the central group; and Preah Stung, two km south-east of the main group, which includes a tower with four faces.

KOH KER កោះកេរ

Koh Ker (also known as Chok Gargyar) served as the capital of Jayavarman IV (ruled 928 to 942) who, having seized the throne, left Angkor and transferred his capital here, where it remained throughout his reign. The principal monument of this large group of interesting ruins is Prasat Thom (also known as Prasat Kompeng), which includes a 40-metre-high, sandstone-faced pyramid of seven levels. Some 40 inscriptions, dating from 932 to 1010, have been found at Prasat Thom.

PREAH VIHEAR ព្រះវិហារ

The important group of Preah Vihear, built on a crest of the Dangkrek Mountains at an altitude of 730 metres, dates from the reign of Suryavarman I (ruled 1002 to 1049). The complex faces south. There are plans to open up the Preah Vihear area to overland tourists from Thailand.

SIEM REAP

For information on Siem Reap and the temples of Angkor, see the Angkor chapter.

Western Cambodia

BATTAMBANG បាត់ដំបង

Battambang, Cambodia's second-largest city and site of a busy market, is built along the Sangker River. In 1970, the population was 40,000; these days, it may be as high as 100,000. Before 1975, places of interest in and around Battambang included: the Pothiveal Museum of Khmer art; Wat Phiphit; Phnom Sampeou Cave; the temples of Prasat Banon, which date from the 12th or 13th century; the temples of Prasat Sneng, which date from the 11th century and are 22 km south of town (towards Pailin); and Prasat Ek Phnom (also known as Wat Ek), eight km north of town, an 11th century site used as a prison by the Khmer Rouge.

Getting There & Away

Land distances from Battambang via National Route 5:

Phnom Penh	292 km
Kompong Chhnang	202 km
Poipet (Thai border)	129 km
Pursat	105 km
Siem Reap	80 km

Kampuchean Airlines have resumed flights between Phnom Penh and Battambang. By rail, Battambang is 274 km from the capital.

PAILIN ប៉ៃលិន

Pailin (elevation 257 metres), 83 km south-west of Battambang near the Thai border, is known for its deposits of white, yellow and black sapphires. Structures of interest in town include Wat Mondul and Wat Phnom Yat, a pagoda built by Shan migrants from Myanmar. Since 1979, there has been bitter fighting in the Pailin area, which has mostly been under Khmer Rouge control.

SISOPHON សិរីសោភ័ណ

There are a number of ruined sanctuaries in the vicinity of Sisophon, which is at the intersection of National Route 5 and National Route 6.

Getting There & Away

Land distances from Sisophon:

Phnom Penh	372 km (National Route 5)
Phnom Penh	414 km (National Route 6)
Battambang	80 km
Kompong Chhnang	282 km
Poipet (Thai border)	49 km
Pursat	185 km
Siem Reap	103 km

Sisophon is on the Phnom Penh-Poipet railway line, which runs through Battambang.

BANTEAY CHHMAR បន្ទាយឆ្មារ

Banteay Chhmar (Narrow Fortress), 71 km north of Sisophon, was one of the capitals of Jayavarman II (ruled 802 to 850). The city, enclosed by a nine-km-long wall, had in its centre one of the largest and most impressive Buddhist monasteries of the Angkor period. The sandstone structure, built in the 11th century and dedicated to Avalokitesvara Bodhisattva, suffered significant damage during repeated Thai invasions, although many of its huge bas-reliefs, which are said to be comparable to those of the Bayon and Angkor Wat, are extant.

POIPET ប៉ោយប៉ែត

Both the rail line and the main road linking Bangkok with Angkor and Phnom Penh pass through the Thai-Cambodian border town of Poipet.

Land distances from Poipet:

Phnom Penh	421 km (National Route 5)
Phnom Penh	463 km (National Route 6)
Siem Reap	152 km
Battambang	129 km
Bangkok	265 km

The Thai border town of Aranyaprathet is five km west of Poipet. By rail, Poipet is 385 km from Phnom Penh and 239 km from Bangkok.

The North-East

All of the provinces along Cambodia's northern border are lightly populated and poorly served by Cambodia's road network.

KRATIE ក្រចេះ
Sites of interest near the riverine town of Kratie, which had a population of 15,000 in the mid-1960s, include the monastery of Phnom Sambok; the Prek Patang Rapids on the Mekong; and Sambor, a 6th and 7th century capital once known as Sambhupura. The monuments of Sambor, which were visited by the Dutchman Van Wusthoff on his way to Vientiane in 1642, consist of eight groups spread over an area of about one sq km.

Getting There & Away
If National Route 7 were open, Kratie would be a 343-km drive from Phnom Penh and a 141-km ride from Stung Treng. Kratie can be reached from the capital by riverboat; the trip takes three days. From Kratie it is possible to go by land eastward to Mondulkiri Province.

STUNG TRENG ស្ទឹងត្រែង
Sites of interest in the vicinity of Stung Treng include the Prek Patang Rapids on the Mekong River and Phnom Chi.

Getting There & Away
Kampuchean Airlines has round trips from Phnom Penh to Stung Treng every Monday.

There are no serviceable land routes between Phnom Penh and Stung Treng; by National Route 7, the distance would be about 484 km. By road, Stung Treng is 217 km from the Lao town of Pakse.

Ferries link Phnom Penh and Kratie with Stung Treng between September and January only.

RATANAKIRI រតនគិរី
Mountainous Ratanakiri Province is home to many of Cambodia's ethno-linguistic minorities, including the groups whose womenfolk are famous for smoking long-stemmed pipes.

Getting There & Away
Because the major bridges on roads between Phnom Penh and Cambodia's far north-eastern province of Ratanakiri are out and have not been replaced by ferries, the area can be reached by land only via the Vietnamese Central Highlands town of Pleiku.

Index

Guides to South-East Asia

South-East Asia on a shoestring
The well-known 'yellow bible' for travellers in South-East Asia covers Brunei, Burma (Myanmar), Cambodia, Hong Kong, Indonesia, Laos, Macau, Malaysia, the Philippines, Singapore, Thailand and Vietnam.

Bali & Lombok - a travel survival kit
This guide will help travellers to experience the real magic of Bali's tropical paradise. Neighbouring Lombok is largely untouched by outside influences and has a special atmosphere of its own.

Burma - a travel survival kit
Burma is one of Asia's most interesting countries. This book shows how to make the most of a trip around the main triangle route of Rangoon–Mandalay–Pagan, and explores many lesser-known places such as Pegu and Inle Lake.

Malaysia, Singapore & Brunei - a travel survival kit
Three independent nations of amazing geographic and cultural variety – from the national parks, beaches, jungles and rivers of Malaysia, tiny oil-rich Brunei and the urban prosperity and diversity of Singapore.

Philippines - a travel survival kit
The friendly Filipinos, colourful festivals, and superb natural scenery make the Philippines one of the most interesting countries in South-East Asia for adventurous travellers and sun-seekers alike.

Indonesia - a travel survival kit
Some of the most remarkable sights and sounds in South-East Asia can be found amongst the 7000 islands of Indonesia – this book covers the entire archipelago in detail.

Hong Kong, Macau & Canton - a travel survival kit
A comprehensive guide to three fascinating cities linked by history, culture and geography.

Thailand - a travel survival kit
This authoritative guide includes Thai script for all place names and the latest travel details for all regions, including tips in trekking in the remote hills of the Golden Triangle.

Vietnam, Laos & Cambodia - a travel survival kit
This comprehensive guidebook has all the information you'll need on this most beautiful region of Asia – finally opening its doors to the world.

Singapore - city guide
Singapore offers a taste of the great Asian cultures in a small, accessible package. This compact guide will help travellers discover the very best that this city of contrasts can offer.

Also available:
Thai phrasebook, *Thai Hill Tribes* phrasebook, *Burmese* phrasebook, *Pilipino* phrasebook, *Indonesian* phrasebook, *Papua New Guinea Pidgin* phrasebook, and *Mandarin Chinese* phrasebook

Where Can You Find Out.........

HOW to get a Laotian visa in Bangkok?

WHERE to go birdwatching in PNG?

WHAT to expect from the police if you're robbed in Peru?

WHEN you can go to see cow races in Australia?

In the Lonely Planet Newsletter!

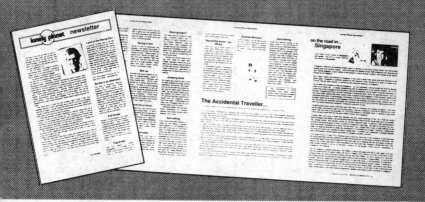

Every issue includes:

- *a letter from Lonely Planet founders Tony and Maureen Wheeler*

- *a letter from an author 'on the road'*

- *the most entertaining or informative reader's letter we've received*

- *the latest news on new and forthcoming releases from Lonely Planet*

- *and all the latest travel news from all over the world*

To receive the FREE quarterly Lonely Planet Newsletter, write to:
Lonely Planet Publications Pty Ltd
PO Box 617, Hawthorn, Vic 3122, Australia
Lonely Planet Publications, Inc
PO Box 2001A, Berkeley, CA 94702, USA

Lonely Planet Guidebooks

Lonely Planet guidebooks cover every accessible part of Asia as well as Australia, the Pacific, South America, Africa, the Middle East and parts of North America and Europe. There are five series: *travel survival kits*, covering a country for a range of budgets; *shoestring guides* with compact information for low-budget travel in a major region; *walking guides*; *city guides* and *phrasebooks*.

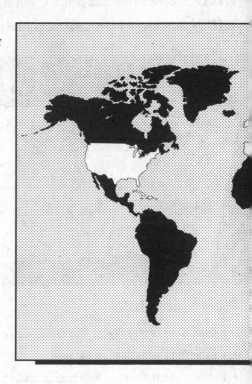

Australia & the Pacific
Australia
Bushwalking in Australia
Islands of Australia's Great Barrier Reef
Fiji
Micronesia
New Caledonia
New Zealand
Tramping in New Zealand
Papua New Guinea
Papua New Guinea phrasebook
Rarotonga & the Cook Islands
Samoa
Solomon Islands
Sydney
Tahiti & French Polynesia
Tonga
Vanuatu

South-East Asia
Bali & Lombok
Burma
Burmese phrasebook
Cambodia
Indonesia
Indonesia phrasebook
Malaysia, Singapore & Brunei
Philippines
Pilipino phrasebook
Singapore
South-East Asia on a shoestring
Thailand
Thai phrasebook
Vietnam, Laos & Cambodia

North-East Asia
China
Mandarin Chinese phrasebook
Hong Kong, Macau & Canton
Japan
Japanese phrasebook
Korea
Korean phrasebook
North-East Asia on a shoestring
Taiwan
Tibet
Tibet phrasebook

West Asia
Trekking in Turkey
Turkey
Turkish phrasebook
West Asia on a shoestring

Middle East
Egypt & the Sudan
Egyptian Arabic phrasebook
Iran
Israel
Jordan & Syria
Yemen

Indian Ocean
Madagascar & Comoros
Maldives & Islands of the East Indian Ocean
Mauritius, Réunion & Seychelles

Mail Order

Lonely Planet guidebooks are distributed worldwide. They are also available by mail order from Lonely Planet, so if you have difficulty finding a title please write to us. US and Canadian residents should write to Embarcadero West, 155 Filbert St, Suite 251, Oakland CA 94607, USA, European residents should write to Devonshire House, 12 Barley Mow Passage, Chiswick, London W4 4PH and residents of other countries to PO Box 617, Hawthorn, Victoria 3122, Australia.

Europe
Eastern Europe on a shoestring
Eastern Europe phrasebook
Iceland, Greenland & the Faroe Islands
Trekking in Spain
USSR
Russian phrasebook

Indian Subcontinent
Bangladesh
India
Hindi/Urdu phrasebook
Trekking in the Indian Himalaya
Karakoram Highway
Kashmir, Ladakh & Zanskar
Nepal
Trekking in the Nepal Himalaya
Nepal phrasebook
Pakistan
Sri Lanka
Sri Lanka phrasebook

Africa
Africa on a shoestring
Central Africa
East Africa
Kenya
Swahili phrasebook
Morocco, Algeria & Tunisia
Moroccan Arabic phrasebook
Zimbabwe, Botswana & Namibia
West Africa

Mexico
Baja California
Mexico

South America
Argentina, Uruguay & Paraguay
Bolivia
Brazil
Brazilian phrasebook
Chile & Easter Island
Colombia
Ecuador & the Galápagos Islands
Latin American Spanish phrasebook
Peru
Quechua phrasebook
South America on a shoestring
Trekking in the Patagonian Andes

Central America
Central America on a shoestring
Costa Rica
La Ruta Maya

North America
Alaska
Canada
Hawaii

The Lonely Planet Story

Lonely Planet published its first book in 1973 in response to the numerous 'How did you do it?' questions Maureen and Tony Wheeler were asked after driving, bussing, hitching, sailing and railing their way from England to Australia.

Written at a kitchen table and hand collated, trimmed and stapled, *Across Asia on the Cheap* became an instant local bestseller, inspiring thoughts of another book.

Eighteen months in South-East Asia resulted in their second guide, *South-East Asia on a shoestring*, which they put together in a backstreet Chinese hotel in Singapore in 1975. The 'yellow bible' as it quickly became known to backpackers around the world, soon became *the* guide to the region. It has sold well over half a million copies and is now in its 7th edition, still retaining its familiar yellow cover.

Today there are over 100 Lonely Planet titles – books that have that same adventurous approach to travel as those early guides; books that 'assume you know how to get your luggage off the carousel' as one reviewer put it.

Although Lonely Planet initially specialised in guides to Asia, they now cover most regions of the world, including the Pacific, South America, Africa, the Middle East and Eastern Europe. The list of *walking guides* and *phrasebooks* (for 'unusual' languages such as Quechua, Swahili, Nepalese and Egyptian Arabic) is also growing rapidly.

The emphasis continues to be on travel for independent travellers. Tony and Maureen still travel for several months of each year and play an active part in the writing, updating and quality control of Lonely Planet's guides.

They have been joined by over 50 authors, 48 staff – mainly editors, cartographers, & designers – at our office in Melbourne, Australia, another 10 at our US office in Oakland, California and have recently opened an office in London. Travellers themselves also make a valuable contribution to the guides through the feedback we receive in thousands of letters each year.

The people at Lonely Planet strongly believe that travellers can make a positive contribution to the countries they visit, both through their appreciation of the countries' culture, wildlife and natural features, and through the money they spend. In addition, the company makes a direct contribution to the countries and regions it covers. Since 1986 a percentage of the income from each book has been donated to ventures such as famine relief in Africa; aid projects in India; agricultural projects in Central America; Greenpeace's efforts to halt French nuclear testing in the Pacific and Amnesty International. In 1991 $68,000 was donated to these causes.

Lonely Planet's basic travel philosophy is summed up in Tony Wheeler's comment, 'Don't worry about whether your trip will work out. Just go!'